What's So Funny?

WIT AND HUMOR IN AMERICAN CHILDREN'S LITERATURE

What's So Funny?

WIT AND HUMOR IN AMERICAN CHILDREN'S LITERATURE

by Michael Cart

HarperCollins*Publishers*

Library of Congress Cataloging-in-Publication Data
Cart, Michael.
    What's so funny? : wit and humor in American children's literature / by Michael Cart.
        p.   cm.
    Includes bibliographical references and index.
    ISBN 0-06-024453-4
    1. Children's literature, American—History and criticism.   2. Humorous stories,
American—History and criticism.   3. Humorous poetry, American—History and
criticism.   4. American wit and humor—History and criticism.   5. Children—
United States—Books and reading.   I. Title
PS490.C37   1995   94-15583
810.9'9282—dc20   CIP
                                                                        AC

Typography by Steven M. Scott
1   2   3   4   5   6   7   8   9   10
❖
First Edition

In memory of

Walter R. Brooks
whose books about Freddy the Pig taught me to laugh

Contents

Foreword

Erich Kästner, the great German humorist, had something of a fetish for forewords. *"Kein Buch ohne Vorwort,"* he once wrote, adding, with sublime logic, *"kein Vorwort ohne Buch!"* ("No book without a foreword . . . no foreword without a book!")

So here we have a foreword, which will be followed, in short order, by a book . . . about humor in children's literature. The scope of the book is American in its geography and post–World War I in its chronology. It is American in part because humor, like certain wines, doesn't always travel well, and thus what may be fall-down-and-roll-around-on-the-floor funny to a German or an Irishman may not elicit so much as a puzzled smile from an

American (and vice versa, of course). It is American in larger part, however, because the world of children's literature is vast, and to try to deal with all of it would require an encyclopedia, not a single volume.

Similarly the time frame covered is a reasonably manageable one: 1920 to date. I have chosen 1920 since that year defines not only the start of the first post–World War I decade but also, in many ways, the dawn of modern children's literature. The stage had been set for this in the two preceding years: In 1918 Anne Carroll Moore, then Head of Children's Work for the New York Public Library, "invented" modern children's book reviewing with her children's page in *The Bookman* magazine, while in 1919 *Children's Book Week* was started and Macmillan became the first publishing house to launch a separate children's book department. The year 1920 saw the publication of Hugh Lofting's *The Story of Doctor Dolittle*, a seminal work in the evolution of children's book humor, since it introduced into works of humor for children a sensibility that is accessible to today's readers. More simply stated, we still find its humor funny, a point worth making, since humor not only doesn't survive travel across geographic boundaries (with few exceptions), it is usually stopped dead at historical borders too. (If you doubt this, try reading some of the "hilarious" work of nineteenth-century humorists like Petroleum V. Nasby or Artemus Ward.)

Two years after the publication of *Dolittle*, the first Newbery Medal was awarded (Lofting's second book, *The Voyages of Doctor Dolittle*, would in 1923 win the second Newbery Medal), and in 1924 *The Horn Book* magazine began publication. Statistics suggest that something significant was happening in the 1920s: In 1919 a total of 433 books for children were published in the United States. By 1929 that number had more than doubled, to

931. "Children," Ruth Hill Viguers noted, had become "individuals in their own right."[1] And the literature published for them had become "individual" in its own right; that is, it had become a separate, identifiable literary genre lending itself to review attention and critical examination.

This book borrows techniques from both fields—reviewing and criticism—and adds to them a certain amount of appreciation and noncritical celebration. And why not? It is written from the point of view of one who passionately believes in the importance of children's books and the reading of them. Sharing one's readerly enthusiasm for truly good books is, I believe, a valid reason for the writing of a book like this.

Humor is full of delightful paradox. One is that people take it *very* seriously. I discovered *how* seriously when word got around among friends and colleagues that I was writing this book. "Well," they would say, their faces suddenly pressed intimidatingly close to mine, "*surely* you're including *my* favorites . . ." and they would proceed to name half a dozen books I had never heard of.

My reply to their demands—which I offer from the safe distance of print—is, "No, I may *not* have included all of your favorites." For this book is not intended to be in any way definitive; the selection of the titles to be discussed is highly personal; the point of view, as noted above, is that of a reviewer and critic and lover of literature for children. The book is not an academic treatise, nor does it dwell on considerations of psychology or anthropology or Marxist economics. The only thing that may be deconstructed is a too-lofty reputation or two. It is as much celebration as it is criticism. Following a first chapter that provides necessary context, the book explores three basic types of humor. One type is universal—the use of talking or otherwise anthropomorphized animals for humorous purpose—while the other two are more singularly American: tall-tale and frontier humor, and what I call domestic or family comedy—the family story being one of the unique contributions of America to the world of children's books. Each of these types utilizes, of course, most of the myriad devices of humor: essential incongruity, frustration of expectation, wit, nonsense, wordplay, satire, slapstick, exaggeration of character and situation; the rude, the polished, the crude, and the polite.

If I have any hope in writing this book, it is that its readers may be inspired to reread and rediscover the works of literature and the authors it discusses, and that that might, in turn, be the occasion for much healthy and healing laughter.

Notes

[1] Viguers, Ruth Hill, "Childhood's Golden Era—Introductory Survey," in Meigs, Cornelia, et al., *A Critical History of Children's Literature*. New York: The Macmillan Co., 1953, p. 437.

Chapter One

....

CONFABULATION AND CONTEXT

....

"One man's meat . . ."

Humor is the Rodney Dangerfield of literary forms: It gets no respect! That something so fundamental to our survival as a species should be so undervalued by the critics and the bestowers of glittering literary prizes is, as Rodgers and Hammerstein's King of Siam put it, "a puzzlement." After all, Rabelais tells us, "Man is the laughing animal."

In fact man is the *only* animal that laughs—probably because man is the only animal that *needs* to laugh. For laughter is the best medicine for melancholy. As Joseph Heller and Norman Cousins have demonstrated in their books *No Laughing Matter* and *Anatomy of an Illness As Perceived by the Patient*, laughter is therapeutic. It is healing. As a tonic for what ails us, it is as potent as—and a whole lot more palatable than—Grandma's proverbial dose of sulfur and molasses. If we hurt, we laugh. And laughing, we heal.

Former *Horn Book* editor Ethel Heins takes this thought one step further, calling laughter not a medicine but "a mechanism for survival,"[1] while clinical child psychologist Martha Wolfenstein—a bit more ponderously—says, "Joking is a gallant attempt to ward off the oppressive difficulties of life, a bit of humble heroism, which, for the moment that it succeeds, provides elation."[2]

Finally, that great observer of children at play Iona Opie says laughter is "the best antidote to the anxieties and disasters of life. . . . A life without it is nothing but an exercise in endurance."[3]

Before we laugh, however, we smile—which suggests that a smile is nothing but a laugh in training wheels! Dr. Martin Grotjahn notes that the smile "is older than laughter" and, as a manifestation of acceptance and pleasure, may appear as early as the eighth day of life. It quickly becomes an exercise in socialization as well. For when the infant and its mother smile at each other, the smile becomes "the first expressive communication between two persons."[4] Take away the mother, and the smile goes away. Remove the mother permanently, and the baby may lose its capacity to smile altogether. Bad news for baby. For, as Dr. Grotjahn asserts, "If the baby has lost its ability to smile, it may be lost for further life and health. The inability to smile characterizes emotional starvation and loss of human contact. . . . It will lead to mental or physical death."[5]

The smile itself doesn't create health and well-being, of course, but it is a passively reliable indicator of it. In terms not of a baby's growth but of our evolution as humans, however, the smile played a more active and vigorous part. A Dutch anthropologist with the wonderful name of J.A.R.A.M. Van Hoof (what do his friends call him, I wonder?) tells us that "the baring of teeth originally formed part of a mainly defensive or protective pattern of behavior."[6]

Later, as we became more civilized, the smile evolved into a still defensive but more sedate "signal of submission and non-hostility." In other words, the smile announces "I'm harmless. Don't hurt me."

And speaking of evolution, the infant's smile, in fairly short order, evolves into the baby's laugh. If, as Dr. Grotjahn reminds us, "the smile is a response to another human being . . . then laughter is a more specialized expression of physical joy and physical contact with the mother. The harmless surprise, Mother's teasing 'boo' is aimed to relieve the baby's unnecessary alarm."[7] Particularly, I would suggest, if it is immediately followed by the mother's smile and hug.

"Surprise" seems to be the key word here. Especially since another early occasion for laughter—the tickle attack—also involves surprise and, like the "boo," is usually followed by the warmth of a reassuring, all's-right-with-the-world hug. Marcel Gutwirth, in his book *Laughing Matter*, suggests the same notion when he writes, "Wired for laughter from birth, we appear to have evolved this capacity to laugh from no other motive than a pleasurable surprise that serves no end but the enjoyment of our own momentary invulnerability in euphoria."[8] (And who is more invulnerable and euphoric than a baby wrapped in a mother's embrace?)

As Gutwirth's word "wired" suggests, laughter seems to be more purely physical than smiling. Smiling is, after all, a controlled response; we can choose to smile and communicate non-verbally thereby. The laugh, on the other hand, is an explosive, involuntary reaction rather like a sneeze—an exercise in release and relief. As human machines our bodies are designed to laugh. A scientist named Michael Duchowny tells us that "neonatal onset—laughter of the newborn—demonstrates that brain substrates for laughter are fully functional at birth."[9]

Gutwirth puts it this way: "Laughter is rooted in our physical makeup and we must therefore look on it as fundamental to human nature."[10]

Now, just as the infant's smile changes to the baby's laugh, so where we look for that fundamental laugh and in what form we seek it will change as *we* continue to change. The sense of humor is developmental. As we grow up, as we mature and become (one hopes) more sophisticated, our sense of humor tends to move from our purely physical viscera to our more cerebral self—from our belly to our brain.

"We could measure our maturity by what makes us laugh," Lloyd Alexander points out.[11]

Tickles, boos, and surprises are replaced, thus, by more sophisticated considerations of incongruity, frustration of expectation, and inventive wordplay. More about those in a moment, but for now a caveat: Beyond noting its chronologically increasing sophistication, it is *very* dangerous to generalize about humor, for "funny" is a relative, not an absolute, term, and an individual's sense of humor is as *individual,* as idiosyncratic, as his or her fingerprints. One person's meat—generously sprinkled with a seasoning of the ineffable—is, you may be sure, another person's poison when humor is sliced and served up.

And so the experts wisely counsel caution when it comes to analyzing what makes us laugh—what it is that triggers that involuntary physical explosion. Here is what popular philosopher, critic, and editor Max Eastman had to say on the subject in his landmark book *The Enjoyment of Laughter*: "All attempts to explain humor have failed . . . because they take humor seriously. They try to explain it . . . and show what its value is as a part of serious life . . . [but] our sense of humor is instinctive [and] the moment anyone approaches a joke with intent to dissect, the joke is dead."[12]

Psychologist Martha Wolfenstein concurs: "To enjoy a joke we must remain unaware of the devices by which it succeeds. On this ground it is sometimes felt that the analysis of the comic is a particularly humorless undertaking."[13]

This sounds, of course, like the kind of cautiously dry analysis that a psychologist might make, but even a great humorist, E. B. White, takes a similarly cautionary and clinical approach: "Humor," he has observed, "can be dissected, as a frog can, but the thing dies in the process and the innards are discouraging to any but the pure scientific mind. . . . Humor has a certain fragility, an evasiveness which one had best respect. Essentially it is a complete mystery."[14]

Well, *that's* encouraging to someone who undertakes the job of writing about humor, isn't it? Yet even if we allow that humor is a mystery, there are plenty of clues to its solution strewn about, and such great "detectives" as the philosophers Aristotle, Plato, Thomas Hobbes, Immanuel Kant, Henri Bergson, Georg Wilhelm Friedrich Hegel, Arthur Schopenhauer, and a clutch of psychologists, psychiatrists, sociologists, anthropologists, and doctors— both medical and academic—have not hesitated to search through them to discover the theoretical whodunit—the why and what of laughter.

Our own investigation of what makes us laugh—or how we might define humor—must start with the world of Classical Antiquity, since our English word "humor" derives from the Latin word *umor*, which meant "liquid," "fluid," or "moisture." As you probably know, the Ancients believed that a person's temperament consisted of four principal fluids, or humors: yellow bile, black bile, blood, and phlegm. Each of these fluids controlled an element of one's temper; for example, yellow bile influenced choler, and black bile, melancholy. Thus, if one's yellow bile content was disproportionately large, one became choleric (i.e., angry or irritable); if one was burdened with too much black bile, one became melancholy, and so forth. A person whose humors were so unbalanced was called a humorist. Both Aristotle and Plato believed that a healthy laugh was a remedy for this situation, since it restored a proper tempermental balance to the "humorist" and served, thus, as a medicine for melancholy (or a cure for choler, if you prefer). One wonders if this is the reason that the phrase "healthy laugh" survives to this day. In any event it took no great leap of semantic imagination thereafter to borrow the word "humorist" from the afflicted and to apply it as well to those who cured the affliction by making the ailing laugh. This notion of humors survived well after the Renaissance and explains, among other things, the significance of the titles of rare Ben Jonson's comedies *Every Man in His Humor* and *Every Man out of His Humor*.

It also explains why some of the earliest theories of humor invoked feelings of superiority or degradation. A person out of his humor was an exercise in exaggeration, even grotesquery—something to feel superior to. Thus the famous lines from Thomas Hobbes: "Sudden glory is the passion which maketh those grimaces called 'laughter.' It arises from a sudden conception of some eminency in ourselves, by comparison with the infirmity of others" (I'm okay, but you're grotesquely out of your humor, ha ha ha!) "or," he continues, "with our own formerly"[15] (I used to be grotesquely out of my humor, but now I'm not, ha ha ha!).

Other philosophers—both before and after Hobbes—who subscribed to what is called the superiority theory of humor include Plato, Aristotle, Cicero, Francis Bacon, René Descartes, Henri Bergson, and Beverly Cleary (!), who, speaking of the genesis of her now-classic character Ramona Quimby, says, "I began to understand that children would enjoy a book about a younger girl because they would recognize and enjoy feeling superior to their younger selves."

When she goes on to say, "Children laugh because they have grown,"[16] she introduces a second aspect of the superiority theory of humor: relief from tension, fear, or anxiety. Here's Max Eastman again: "The things we laugh at are awful while they are going on, but get funny when we look back."[17]

So if it is funny to see someone slip on a banana peel because we feel superior to the slipper, it may be twice as funny if we ourselves have previously slipped on the same banana peel but are now too deft and dexterous to do so again.

Though we today dismiss ideas of liquid humors controlling our temperaments, aspects of this notion continue to influence our thinking about humor. For example: Characters who are humorous because of their eccentricities or exaggerated characteristics are as funny in our day as they were in Ben Jonson's (my guess is that he would find Harry Allard's Stupids, Helen Cresswell's Bagthorpes, or Lucretia Hale's Peterkins as funny as we contemporary readers do).

More subtly, however, this notion of liquid humors may explain, at least in part, why we traditionally tend to undervalue humor in our literature. Tragedy, after all—at least according to Aristotle in his *Poetics*—was an imitation of "an action of high importance, complete, and of some amplitude."[18] It often involved characters of exalted station who, through their hubris, found themselves in conflict with the gods. And we know who will lose not only that battle but—in Classical tragedy, at least—their lives, as well.

Humor, on the other hand, dealt in human grotesquery, in scenes featuring some bilious guy dropping his pants! No wonder Lloyd Alexander recalls having felt vaguely insulted the first time he was called a humorist.

Humor is the loser even when compared with its alleged ally, wit. For apparently that which originates in our physical beings or the situations in which we find them is viewed as less valuable than that which is more clearly cerebral. Slapstick, the most physical type of slip-on-a-banana-peel humor, is less highly regarded than an elegant Oscar Wilde epigram. This would suggest that wit, the product of an active mind at play, is to be valued more than humor, which is the product of active—er—viscera at play. And yet those who value humanity may disagree. Lloyd Alexander, for example, makes a nice distinction between the two. "Wit," he says, "deals with ideas and humor deals with humanity. Wit is laughter of the mind; humor is laughter of the heart."[19]

Another critic simply dismisses wit as being "primarily cleverness and thus without passion or heart," adding, "Wit surprised the mind but humour was more delightful and appealed to the heart as well."[20]

The issue may be moot in this context, however, since all literary humor, at least, involves some kind of "elevating" mental activity. Anthropologist Mahadev Apte calls humor "a cognitive, often unconscious experience involving internal redefining of sociocultural reality and resulting in a mirthful state of mind."[21]

Whatever relative value we assign to humor or wit, it seems inarguable that the appreciation of the latter requires greater maturity than certain elementary forms of the former. Writing in *Library Quarterly*, Katherine Kappas notes that "visual forms of humor generally dominate until the child reaches high school [hence, I would point out, the plethora of humorous picture books], when verbal humor and wit begin to command increasing attention and gradually become the major forms of humorous behavior."[22]

Similarly the appreciation of the humor of incongruity (the matching of two generally accepted incompatibles) or the closely related frustration of expectation require a certain degree of maturity, too; i.e., if we are to find humor in incompatibles or in the frustration of our expectations, we must first occupy a world large enough to recognize incompatibles when they are paired (Walter R. Brooks's Freddy the Pig riding a bicycle, for example, or—a triple incongruity, since he is a male American pig—disguised in a dress as an Irish washerwoman!). Or we need to be experienced enough to have certain expectations of cause and effect, so we can laugh when they are frustrated. For example, we might laugh if a magician reached into his tall silk hat and pulled out . . . nothing (we are conditioned to expect him to pull out a rabbit), but we would also laugh—perhaps even more heartily—if, à la Bullwinkle the Moose of the *Rocky and Bullwinkle* TV show, he reached into the hat and pulled out not a rabbit but an angry tiger, instead. We laugh too at the further incongruity of a moose as a magician, and also because the cartoonist who has created Bullwinkle has, through exaggeration and caricature, made him funny to look at.

Incongruity and frustration of expectation offer common ground to both humor and wit. Max Eastman says they "spring a neat practical joke upon a playful mind."[23]

A practical joke involves an element of surprise. And surprising the mind seems to be at the—well, *heart* of incongruous humor and frustrated expectation. When you add the element of anticipation to this, you bring in literary considerations of pacing and timing and invoke the same pleasurable mind-set kids enjoy five minutes before recess.

Walter R. Brooks was a master of creating such anticipation. In *Wiggins for President* (Knopf, 1939), for example, he takes fourteen pages to get Freddy onto a bicycle so that he can have him fall off in the space of a short paragraph! The anticipation of this denouement is delicious, but it would also be funny if our expectation were frustrated by Freddy's turning out, improbably, to be a master cyclist.

This tripartite parcel—incongruity, surprise, and frustrated expectation—comprises the second major theory of humor (superiority and degradation being the first, remember). Its principal proponents include Kant, Schopenhauer, Hegel, Bergson, and—yes—Brooks!

The third principal theory of humor, relief of tension, is basically Sigmund Freud's private reserve: He called it "outwitting the censor." This kind of humor, the late Alvin Schwartz has pointed out, satisfies our basic needs "for pleasure and for release."[24] It is the forbidden kind of dirty-word, scatological (bathroom), or sexual humor that is more likely to be greeted with a snigger than with a laugh.

Roald Dahl knew how popular this kind of forbidden humor is and took many trips to the bank because of it. Betsy Byars is not the practitioner that Dahl was, but she also understands its popularity.

"The forbidden is always funny," she notes in her 1992 Zena Sutherland Lecture, "and usually the first kind of humor that kids discover is bathroom humor, and all too often the appetite for this kind of humor is lifelong."

For those who might wonder, Mrs. Byars helpfully points out that "the funniest word in the vocabulary of a second grader is 'underwear.'"[25]

Two recent examples of books employing this kind of subversive or forbidden school-yard humor are Tony Ross's *I Want My Potty* (Kane/Miller, 1986) and the new edition of Iona and Peter Opie's classic collection of rhymes, riddles, and chants, *I Saw Esau* (Candlewick, 1992), which is graced with equally subversive illustrations by the great Maurice Sendak. Here's a sample verse:

> Quick! quick!
> The cat's been sick.
>
> Where? where?
> Under the chair.
>
> Hasten! hasten!
> Fetch the basin.
>
> Alack! alack!
>   It is too late.
> The carpet's in
>   An awful state.
>
> No! no!
>   It's all in vain.
> For she has licked it
>   Up again.

It's amazing how these rhymes travel. I learned a shorter and less elegant version of this when I was a in grade school myself in Logansport, Indiana, in the 1940s:

Hasten, Jason,
Bring the basin.

Urp, slop!
Bring the mop.

Happily, life is more gloriously complex than these subversively simple rhymes would suggest. And humor, in practice, does not always lend itself to the neat theoretical compartmentalizations we have posited above. The joyous pleasure of laughter, not the tedious analysis of what engendered the physical act, is ultimately the glory of humor. In fact, the best kinds of humorous books, for children or adults, will probably employ both wit and humor; anticipation and expectation; superiority and inferiority; subversion, slapstick, and subtlety; and frustration and fulfillment. They will appeal, thus, to the fully developed, integrated sense of humor. Such a sense of humor "signifies emotional maturity," Grotjahn tells us. "Humor is the final integration of all stages . . . [when the individual] can be good, tolerant, and accepting of himself and therefore of other people, too."[26]

This process of integration is, essentially, the process of growing up. As Katherine Kappas tells us, "Considerable evidence supports the view that the formation of a sense of humor follows a general developmental pattern and that this pattern parallels and is dependent upon the child's intellectual and emotional development."[27]

Ms. Kappas goes on to identify ten basic categories or types of humor that will appeal to the child at various stages of its development and that will be found, individually or in combination, in most humorous children's books. They are:

1. Exaggeration or hyperbole. The inspiration for America's unique contribution to the world of humor, the tall tale and the larger-than-life American folk hero: Davy Crockett, Paul Bunyan, and others.
2. Incongruity.
3. Surprise.
4. Slapstick.
5. The absurd. This includes whimsy and nonsense, the stuff of Dr. Seuss and Edward Lear.
6. Human predicaments, including situation comedy and humor of superiority and degradation. Look for Beverly Cleary's Ramona Quimby and Lois Lowry's Anastasia Krupnik here.
7. Ridicule.
8. Defiance.
9. Violence. These last three are the province of Freud; the grisly "Struwwelpeter," Heinrich Hoffman's cautionary tales first published in Germany in 1845; and, of course, the incorrigible Roald Dahl.
10. Verbal humor. While, as we have noted, the appreciation of this kind of humor requires a certain maturity, Alvin Schwartz has reminded us that "a fair amount of the joking children do [does] involve word play."[28] Much of the humor of Peggy Parrish's Amelia Bedelia, for example, derives from Amelia's slavishly literal interpretations of words and phrases—not only an example of verbal humor but a wonderful opportunity for very small children to savor the humor of superiority. This is also the reason why riddles (*pace* Dr. Freud) are so precious to kids five to eleven. Knowing the answer lets them feel superior to both their peers and—even better—adults!

The most satisfying humor is obviously a portmanteau device that incorporates a delightful variety of lighthearted elements. Ultimately it is a playful way of looking at the world. As Beverly Cleary notes, "Humor must spring from a writer's view of life."[29]

The point from which life is viewed requires a certain amount of distance, though. Consider what Max Eastman says: "In everything that we do perceive as funny there is an element which, if we were serious and sufficiently sensitive and sufficiently concerned, would be unpleasant."[30] We find Betsy Byars's character Bingo Brown and his problems with love hilarious. But if *we* were Bingo and if, instead of being buffered by the distance of fiction, *we* were experiencing his problems and frustrations in real life, our experience would be not only unpleasant but acutely painful. In that sense, literary humor offers a distancing from pain that is, in short, essential to existence.

Wolfenstein again: "While the particular exigencies which joking aims to alleviate vary with age, the basic motive of briefly triumphing over distress, of gaining a momentary release from frustration persists . . . thus, humor remains a beneficent resource. Only complete omnipotence could dispense with it."[31]

Children are no more omnipotent than adults. Happily, the resource kids require is ready at hand, in the great body of humorous children's literature.

In fact, the very size of that body is a problem for the critic. Ultimately the strategy I have evolved for dealing with it, as noted in the Foreword, is to focus on three specific types of humorous books: Two are quintessentially American, and one is universal. The American types are 1) hyperbole and tall-tale humor and 2) domestic or family comedy, rooted in *Little Women* and evolving through the *Five Little Peppers* and Eleanor Estes's Moffat family to the contemporary Beverly Cleary and her Ramona Quimby,

Betsy Byars's Blossom family, and Lois Lowry's Anastasia Krupnik.

It is the third, however—the universal type—that I want to look at first. It is also the oldest type, and it is, of course, talking-animal humor.

Notes

[1]Heins, Ethel, "A Cry for Laughter." *The Horn Book*, LV:631 (December 1979).

[2]Wolfenstein, Martha S., *Children's Humor: A Psychological Analysis.* Bloomington: Indiana University Press, 1978, p. 11.

[3]Opie, Iona and Peter, eds., *I Saw Esau.* Cambridge, Mass.: Candlewick Press, 1992, p. 14.

[4]Grotjahn, Martin, *Beyond Laughter.* New York: McGraw-Hill Book Co., Inc., 1957, p. 74.

[5]Grotjahn, pp. 68–69.

[6]Van Hoof, J.A.R.A.M., "A Comparative Approach to the Philogeny of Laughter and Smiling." Quoted in Marcel Gutwirth, *Laughing Matter.* Ithaca, N.Y.: Cornell University Press, 1993, p. 5.

[7]Grotjahn, p. 74.

[8]Gutwirth, Marcel, *Laughing Matter.* Ithaca, N.Y.: Cornell University Press, 1993, p. 15.

[9]Duchowny, Michael S., "Pathological Disorders of Laughter." Quoted in Gutwirth, p. 8.

[10]Gutwirth, p. 8.

[11]Alexander, Lloyd, "No Laughter in Heaven." *The Horn Book*, XLVI:17 (February 1970).

[12]Eastman, Max, *Enjoyment of Laughter.* New York: Simon & Schuster, 1936, pp. 15, 26, 42.

[13]Wolfenstein, p. 7.

[14]White, E. B., and Katharine S. White, eds., *A Subtreasury of American Humor.* New York: The Modern Library, 1941, pp. xvii–xviii.

[15]Hobbes, Thomas, *Leviathan.* Edited with an introduction by Michael Oakeshott. Oxford: Basil Blackwell, 1960, p. 36.

[16]Cleary, Beverly, "The Laughter of Children." *The Horn Book*, LVIII:561 (October 1982).

[17]Eastman, p. 341.

[18]Beckson, Karl, and Arthur Ganz, *Literary Terms: A Dictionary*. New York: The Noonday Press, 1989, p. 284.

[19]Alexander, p. 12.

[20]Tave, Stuart Malcolm, "Humour," in *Encyclopedia Britannica*, 11:840. Chicago: Encyclopedia Britannica, Inc., 1972.

[21]Apte, Mahadev L., *Humor and Laughter*. Ithaca, N.Y.: Cornell University Press, 1985, p. 14.

[22]Kappas, Katharine H., "A Developmental Analysis of Children's Responses to Humor." *The Library Quarterly*, 37:70 (January 1967).

[23]Eastman, p. 60.

[24]Schwartz, Alvin, "Children, Humor and Folklore, Part I." *The Horn Book*, LIII:283 (June 1977).

[25]Byars, Betsy, "Taking Humor Seriously," in *The Zena Sutherland Lectures: 1983–1992*, edited by Betsy Hearne. New York: Clarion Books, 1993, p. 216.

[26]Grotjahn, p. 81.

[27]Kappas, p. 69.

[28]Schwartz, p. 283.

[29]Cleary, p. 557.

[30]Eastman, p. 21.

[31]Wolfenstein, p. 12.

Chapter Two

....

ANIMALS AND OTHERS

....

"This is a funny world. And we humans, I often think,
are the funniest animals in it."
"Why, bless me, you can talk to the bloomin' animals."
—Doctor Dolittle's Circus *by Hugh Lofting*

The use of animals for humorous effect—either as beings true to their essential animal natures or, more typically, as anthropomorphized human surrogates—is as old as Aesop. Their primal place in literature for children is due in part, of course, to kids' natural love for creatures with fur and feathers, but in larger part it is due to authors' understanding that most kids are not mature enough to laugh at themselves, the necessary distance of age and the framework of experience having not yet visited their lives. Put the kids into an animal skin, however, and there is suddenly enough margin for mirth. Let them, further, do something recognizably, *humanly* foolish, something that satirizes the social order or—best of all—is downright subversive, undermining adult authority, and joy is unconfined.

Satire and superiority are, thus, mainstays of humorous animal fiction. But they are by no means the only types of humorous devices employed, nor can they begin to describe the scope of their authors' humorous worldviews. The greatest practitioners of funny animal fiction—Hugh Lofting, Walter R. Brooks, Robert Lawson, and Arnold Lobel, among others—are positively polymath in the varieties of humorous devices at their disposal and in their endlessly inventive capacity for bringing delightful disorder to an orderly world and then, after a deeply satisfying adventure, restoring order to that same world now enriched by the experience.

The Story of Doctor Dolittle, published in 1920, is a not-atypical example of this pattern, but in its use of humor accessible to modern readers, its respect for the intelligence of its audience, and its introduction of one of the great characters of children's literature, it is a groundbreaking work.

Its author, Hugh Lofting, was born January 14, 1886, at Maidenhead in Berkshire, England. What, then, is he doing in a book about American children's literature? The same problem, in reverse, confronted English critic Frank Eyre: "I feel a little uneasy about claiming Hugh Lofting as a British children's writer . . ." he admitted in his book *British Children's Books in the Twentieth Century.*[1]

Our mutual problem is that while Lofting was born and raised in England, he was educated, at least in part, in the United States (he studied at the Massachusetts Institute of Technology in 1904–5) and, after completing his education at the London Polytechnic, ultimately returned to the United States in 1912. He subsequently

became a naturalized American citizen and lived the rest of his life
in this country, dying in Santa Monica, California, in 1947. In biographical terms he may thus be considered both British and American, though his biographer, Edward Blishen, states, "Americans will
forgive me for saying that Hugh Lofting, for all his years of resi-
dence, never really became an American. (He kept, all his life, his
British citizenship.)"[2]

Nevertheless all of his major works—including the Doctor
Dolittle books—were first published in the United States (indeed,
the second Dolittle book, *The Voyages of Doctor Dolittle*, won
America's highest children's book award, the Newbery Medal, in
1923) and are, accordingly, part of the great body of American
children's literature. (And besides, the literary life is full of
such amusing anomalies. Rudyard Kipling's *Jungle Books* were
written not in India or even in England but, rather, in Brattleboro,
Vermont!)

Eyre's take on this dilemma, that "whatever nation claims
Lofting he is one of the true internationals of children's writers . . ."
may be a too-easy equivocation, but it is inarguably true and interestingly consistent with what would be Lofting's own political
philosophy. Blishen points out that he had "a passionate longing
for international sanity"[3] and, in corroboration, offers the following from Lofting himself: "If we make children see that all races,
given equal physical and mental chances for development, have
about the same batting averages of good and bad, we shall have
laid another very substantial foundation stone in the edifice of
peace and internationalism."[4]

This longing translated into a growing pacifism, which found
its finest expression not in Lofting's tendentious adult poem "Victory for the Slain," published in 1942, but in the peaceable king-
dom that Dr. Dolittle creates through his medical ministrations to

the animals and through his capacity to communicate with and learn from them.

Despite Lofting's internationalism and pacifism, parts of his work are inarguably offensive to today's readers, since they reflect the colonial attitudes of his British boyhood when, as critic John Rowe Townsend puts it, "all foreigners were funny and those of a different colour were doubly funny."[5]

Lofting's treatment of African characters, as epitomized by the malapropism-spouting Prince Bumpo, is considered particularly offensive by observers like librarian Isabelle Suhl, who calls Lofting a "white racist and chauvinist, guilty of almost every prejudice known to modern white Western man."[6]

Suhl is also critical of Lofting's characterization of the Indians of Popsipetal (in *The Voyages of Doctor Dolittle*) as being childlike.

Lofting's current American publisher, Delacorte Press, attempted to deal with this controversy by issuing, in the late 1980s, new editions of the Dolittle books. In them passages and incidents deemed offensive were deleted.

Lofting's son, Christopher, defended this decision in his Afterword, writing, "Hugh Lofting would have been appalled at the suggestion that any part of his work could give offense and would have been the first to have made the changes himself."[7]

I suspect that is true and I agree with Townsend when he notes, "It is sad that a writer with such excellent intentions should have got himself into such posthumous trouble. I hope that in time Lofting will be forgiven, for assuredly there was no malice in this worried, sincere, well-meaning man."[8]

Lofting's essential compassion is evidenced, I believe, by the genesis of *The Story of Doctor Dolittle*.

It was written in the trenches of World War I, beginning—in the tradition of Kenneth Grahame and Beatrix Potter—as letters to children, in this case, Lofting's own: "My children at home wanted letters from me. . . . There seemed very little of interest to write to youngsters from the front; the news was either too horrible or [too] dull. . . . One thing, however, that kept forcing itself more and more on my attention was the very considerable part the animals were playing in the world war. . . . If we made the animals take the same chances we did ourselves, why did we not give them similar attention when wounded? But obviously to develop a horse surgery as good as that of our Casualty Clearing Station would necessitate a knowledge of horse language. . . . "[9]

It would also necessitate the creation of a medical man who would prefer an animal practice to a more lucrative human one. Enter John Dolittle, M.D., of Puddleby-on-the-Marsh. ("'M.D.,'" Lofting tells us, "means that he was a proper doctor and knew a whole lot" [p. 1].)

The Doctor was, in some ways, a typical Englishman. Like his creator, Lofting, he was, for example, "very fond of animals" (p. 2). In itself this fondness has little humorous possibility. However, when exaggerated, it enables Lofting to turn the Doctor into another kind of typical Englishman and comic type: the eccentric, a man out of his humor, a man who may be considered, well, *unbalanced* by more sedate society. Thus the Doctor is not simply fond of animals, but "had rabbits in the pantry, white mice in his piano, [and] a squirrel in the linen closet . . ." (p. 2). Lofting went him one better in this regard: As a boy, he kept "a combination zoo and natural history museum" in his mother's linen closet.[10]

The Doctor's love for animals offers Lofting not only opportunity for the humor of exaggeration but also for irony, as the Doctor's loving kindness toward animals does not result in reward but rather, as it grows to grander, ever more exaggerated proportions, in the loss of his human clientele, sometimes precipitously: "And one day when an old lady with rheumatism came to see the Doctor, she sat on the hedgehog who was sleeping on the sofa and never came to see him any more . . ." (pp. 2–3).

Irony turns into satire when the Doctor is confronted by his sharp-tongued sister, Sarah: "If you go on like this, none of the best people will have you for a doctor."

The Doctor's reply: "But I like the animals better than the 'best people.'"

"'You are ridiculous,' said his sister, and walked out of the room"(p. 4).

Sarah here is the voice of the real (i.e., adult) world, which would find ridiculous a man who prefers animals to the "best" people. Children will understand why the Doctor prefers the animal world to the "real" world, and if they have any lingering doubts, Lofting offers them this acidic insight through the voice of Miranda, the Purple Bird of Paradise: "it's as much as your life is worth to go near most humans—They say, 'oh how pretty!' and shoot an arrow or a bullet into you" (*Voyages*, p. 132).

Sarah would not understand this, of course, and it is a further satirical indictment that she is not alone, for, as noted, the Doctor has fewer and fewer human patients and gets poorer and poorer as a result, until he has only one patient left: Matthew Muggs, the vaguely larcenous Cat's-meat-Man who "wasn't very rich and he only got sick once a year—at Christmas-time, when he used to give the Doctor sixpence for a bottle of medicine.

"Sixpence a year wasn't enough to live on . . ." (*Story*, p. 5).

The last sentence is an example of the delicious humor of understatement, which will be a leitmotif in the Dolittle books, as will the Doctor's naïve attitude toward material means: "What does money matter, so long as we are happy?" he asks innocently (p. 24). When it is brought forcibly to his attention that *some* money is required for some enterprise or other in which he is interested (a voyage, usually), his reply is typically, "What a nuisance money is, to be sure!" (p. 31).

This attitude toward money is also demonstrated in his comic incapacity to manage it, and so it is left to the animals, who are innately more practical (i.e., adult), to manage it for him. And it is usually Dab-Dab, the Doctor's duck housekeeper, who offers ironic or sarcastic comment on this. For example, when the Doctor says (on p. 84), "But I don't want any money," Dab-Dab's sharp reply is, "Oh, do be sensible!" (p. 86). On another occasion, she is more resigned: "'Oh, dear!' sighed the duck. 'Did anyone ever see a man who could find so many objections to getting rich?'" (*Doctor Dolittle's Post Office*, 1923, p. 286). Later in the same book: "There goes the Dolittle fortune," Dab-Dab says. "My, but it is marvelous how money *doesn't* stick to that man's fingers!" The reply of the Doctor's pet pig, Gub-Gub, is telling: "Easy comes, easy goes. Never mind. I don't suppose it's really such fun being rich. Wealthy people have to behave so unnaturally" (p. 309).

It is not just wealthy people who behave unnaturally, however, but the human race as a whole that has been forced into grotesque (and therefore laughable) unnaturalness by the dictates of "civilization." Animals, by contrast, behave naturally by being true to their essential animal natures and are, thus, wiser than humans. Some of them are quick to point this out: Polynesia, the cantankerous parrot: "Be an animal-doctor," she counsels John Dolittle. "Give the silly people up—if they haven't brains enough to see you're the best doctor in the world. Take care of animals instead—*they*'ll soon find it out" (*Story*, p. 9).

Even the generally mild-mannered Doctor can, when provoked, be harshly critical of humans too: "The animal sense of humor is far superior to the human," he explains to Matthew Muggs in *Doctor Dolittle's Circus* (1924). "But people are too stupid to see the funniness of things that animals do to amuse one another. And in most cases I have to bring them down to our level—to have them make their style of jokes rather— er—crude and broad. Otherwise people mightn't understand them at all" (p. 378).

The animals can, themselves, become the object of humor if they assume attitudes that are too human (i.e., flawed). For example, when circumstance takes the Doctor and his household to Africa for the first time (in *Story*), the Doctor is thwarted in his efforts to enlist the jungle animals' help in curing a plague that is devastating the monkey population, because the lion, the King of Beasts, is too . . . *imperial* in his attitude:

"But the leader of the lions was a very proud creature. . . .

"'Do you dare to ask me—*ME, the king of beasts*, to wait on a lot of dirty monkeys? Why, I wouldn't even eat them between meals!'"

The Doctor's reply is mild but devastating: "I didn't ask you to eat them. And besides, they're not dirty. They've all had a bath this morning. *Your* coat looks as though it needed brushing—badly" (p. 69).

Then, when the lion proudly tells his wife what he has done, the lioness—beside herself with worry because her two cubs are ill—calls her husband a "great booby" and pulls his hair (p. 72).

In the end the lion must swallow his pride and help the Doctor.

The lion, of course, is a minor, one-dimensional character. The major animal characters—particularly the permanent members of the Doctor's household: Jip the dog, Dab-Dab the duck, Gub-Gub the pig, Polynesia the parrot, and others—provide a more interesting problem. Given the gift of speech, they automatically assume, in the reader's mind, human aspects. How does one balance their animal natures with the inevitable anthropomorphism?

Margery Fisher speaks for most critics when she says, "Hugh Lofting established his animal characters on several levels. First, they are never less than their natural selves: Jip's acute nose, Gub-Gub's greed . . . are true to the facts of animal behavior. Secondly, they operate, physically and mentally, in the world of humans—that is, they perform roles which seem natural because of our traditional beliefs about their animal natures."[11]

In other words, the animals are *congruous*. Polynesia the parrot is a good example of this: Parrots are talking birds; accordingly it makes sense that it should be she who teaches the Doctor how to speak animal languages—a delightful notion but not intrinsically humorous. The humor comes in the fact that Polynesia not only talks, she never shuts her sharp-tongued, opinionated beak!

Too-Too, the owl, provides an even better example of Ms. Fisher's points: Because he is an owl, we expect him to be wise, and so he is made by Lofting to be a great mathematician, responsible for the household accounts, for the post office's bookkeeping requirements, and so on. In his physical being as an owl, Too-Too also has acute hearing. What Lofting does with this is typical of his humorous spin on the facts of natural history. Not only does Too-Too have acute hearing, he has *extraordinarily* acute hearing: "But we owls can tell you, using only one ear, the color of a kitten from the way it winks in the dark" (*Story*, p. 137).

Similarly, Jip as a dog is faithful, genial, and bluff. In his physical being he has an acute sense of smell—*extraordinarily* acute: "'Does hot water have a smell?' asked the Doctor.

"'Certainly it has,' said Jip. 'Hot water smells quite different from cold water. It is warm water—or ice—that has the really difficult smell'" (*Story*, p. 155).

Dab-Dab the duck is perhaps the least successful example of this duality, since she is one of the most heavily anthropomorphized of the animals. Indeed, she is far less duck than fussy, middle-aged Englishwoman. This is due, in large part, to the role Lofting has assigned her: the Doctor's housekeeper. As such she must sweep floors, make beds, air linens, and perform prodigies of other most unducklike physical activities.

Gub-Gub, the pig, is even more heavily anthropomorphized, although he *is* faithful to his porcine nature in his greed. "You always think of things to eat," Jip grouses (*Story*, p. 157). Dab-Dab's attitude toward this is predictably fussy: Complaining that Gub-Gub is trying to be funny most of the time, she asserts, "Eating is not a matter to be played with and joked about. It is a serious subject" (*Gub Gub's Book*, 1932, p. 5).*

Perhaps because Gub-Gub is the most human of all the animals, he is also the most childish, being, for the most part, simply a little boy dressed up in a pig suit (little boys, the last time I looked, are also greedy!). Too-Too observes, "That pig . . . reminds me of a boy I knew once. A small boy with a large appetite . . ." (*Gub Gub's Book*, p. 13).

This gives Lofting two reliable opportunities for humor: one is physical. Gub-Gub's greed, curiosity, and "boyish" impetuousness are forever getting him into scrapes: He gets stuck by the pushmi-pullyu's horns when the animals play *Hunt-the-Slipper*, for example; on another occasion he gets "all worked up" when the Doctor dives for pearls, and "before anybody could stop him *he* had taken a plunge." Of course, "he got his snout stuck in the mud at the bottom, and the Doctor, still out of breath, had to go down

---

*For some reason Lofting spelled both Dab Dab's and Gub Gub's names without their customary hyphens in this one volume.

after him and get him free" (*Post Office*, p. 285).

In *Doctor Dolittle's Circus* we are amused to learn that "Gub-Gub's luggage was a bundle of turnips; and just as he was hurrying down the steps to the road the string broke and the round, white vegetables went rolling all over the place" (p. 25).

Gub-Gub's childishness often causes problems for the other animals. In *Story*, for example, when the animals get lost in the jungle, Polynesia rants, "It was all that stupid pig's fault. He would keep running off the path hunting for ginger-roots. And I was kept so busy catching him and bringing him back, that I turned to the left, instead of the right, when we reached the swamp" (p. 95). (There is an element of truth in this, of course, but Polynesia's defensive bluster makes us smile in recognition of her own dereliction.)

Most often, though, the pig simply provides a convenient target for the other animals' invective and epithet. Cheapside the sparrow calls him "Perfesser Bacon" and "Doctor Hog" (*Gub Gub's Book*, pp. 14 and 56). Jip calls him "you stupid piece of warm bacon" (*Story*, p. 153). Dab-Dab sputters, "You—you—sausage!" (*Circus*, p. 153). Taken out of context, these epithets can sound cruel and sarcastic, and indeed, aimed at a more sensitive target, they could wound. Gub-Gub, however, seems to be blithely unaware that he is being insulted. Like a child, he is totally egocentric, self-absorbed, and self-important. Here is the pig as self-styled author: "'[Olives] upset my temperament.' 'What might that be?' asked the White Mouse. 'I'm not quite sure. . . . But it is something all authors have. Don't interrupt'" (*Gub Gub's Book*, p. 33).

And again, when he plays the part of Pantaloon in an animal theatrical production and comes upon a picture of himself on a poster, "He would have sat in front of it all night, if [the other animals] had let him, admiring himself as a famous actor" (*Circus*, p. 326). On the rare occasions when he does reply to the other animals' invective, the result is only another joke at his expense: "'Please don't call me "hog,"' said Gub Gub peevishly. 'I wish you would remember that I have a pedigree—a long pedigree.'

"'A short tail and long pedigree!'" the White Mouse whispers, "tittering over his own joke" (*Gub Gub's Book*, pp. 56–57).

While the other animals may grow impatient with Gub-Gub, one suspects that Lofting never did. The pig is, after all, the only one of the animals to have his own book (the eponymous *Gub Gub's Book*, published in 1932). The careful reader may suspect that this title not only gives Lofting a chance to indulge his (arguably) favorite animal character but himself as well, since the book allows him to create an uncommonly large number of the excruciatingly bad puns that are a humorous staple of all the Dolittle books.

"'Fat you may be,' snorted Dab Dab [to Gub Gub]. 'But what should make you *fat*igued?'" (p. 16).

"After all," Gub-Gub asserts grandly, "I do my best to enlighten your ignorance." Jip, without missing a beat, replies, "Our *pig*norance, you mean" (p. 51).

On another occasion the Doctor pronounces an opossum "One of the marsupials." Gub-Gub replies (loudly enough to be heard over the grinding of the reader's teeth), "How do you know it's a Ma Soupial, Doctor? She hasn't any children with her. Perhaps, it's a Pa Soupial" (*Circus*, p. 32).

There is something of the English music hall in the Dolittle books. Their tone can be jokey (especially in *Gub Gub's Book*— "I'll tell you more another night. It is the hour for my bibliography. I must go and bibble" [p. 23]) and their humor crude and broad (remember the old lady and the hedgehog?). Slapstick is certainly a regular visitor to the texts, and the Doctor himself is sometimes the target. "Lor' bless us, Doctor," Cheapside observes, "but you do get yourself into some comical situations! . . . 'Elp the Doctor up, Jip. Look, 'e's got his chin caught under a root" (*Post Office*, p. 324). Another time an honest sailor mistakes the Doctor for a pirate and "began to punch the Doctor in the dark." Happily, the Doctor is not hurt badly, "because it was too dark to punch properly" (*Story*, p. 167).

At the other end of the humorous spectrum is the understatement mentioned earlier, which provides both reliable relief from the cruder humor and helps establish character, particularly the Doctor's. Consider: The Doctor is tossed into a windowless prison with his hands "firmly tied behind his back with strong rope.

"'Dear me,' said he . . . 'what a poor holiday I am spending, to be sure!'" (*Post Office*, p. 293). On another occasion, his ship sinking under him in the midst of a terrible storm, the Doctor's strongest reaction is a mild, "We must have run into Africa. Dear me, dear me!" (*Story*, p. 40). Or: "So the Doctor and his pets were led back to prison and locked up. . . .

"They were all very unhappy.

"'This is a great nuisance,' said the Doctor" (*Story*, p. 93).

Slapstick and understatement are often combined, to good comedic effect: the Doctor has temporarily (and inadvertently) bested a band of pirates who are left bobbing helplessly in the bay. Jip keeps snapping at their noses "so they were afraid to climb up the side of [the Doctor's] ship." The physical humor of the situation having been brilliantly realized, Lofting proceeds to expand its comic possibilities by producing a school of sharks. The pirates cry, "Help, help!—The sharks! The sharks!"

They have good reason to be concerned. One of the sharks,

approaching the Doctor, offers to help: "we know these pirates to be a bad lot . . ." he says. "If they are annoying you, we will gladly eat them up for you. . . ." The Doctor's reply is memorable in its delicious understatement: "Thank you," he says. "This is really most attentive" (*Story*, pp. 129–30). (He declines the offer, of course.)

A personal favorite example of the mixture of slapstick and understatement occurs in *The Voyages of Doctor Dolittle*, when the adventurers are departing on their voyage to Spider Monkey Island. Here is how the Doctor's secretary, Tommy Stubbins, describes it: "We bumped into one or two other boats getting out into the stream; and at one sharp bend in the river we got stuck on a mud bank for a few minutes. But though the people on the shore seemed to get very excited at these things, the Doctor did not appear to be disturbed by them in the least.

"'These little accidents will happen in the most carefully regulated voyages,' he said as he leaned over the side and fished for his boots which had gotten stuck in the mud while we were pushing off. 'Sailing is much easier when you get out into the open sea. There aren't so many silly things to bump into'" (pp. 152–53).

Another instance of understatement offers a definitive aspect of the Doctor's character: In *Story*, the Doctor, having lost the ship in which he sailed to Africa, wonders "where we are going to get another boat to go home in. . . . Oh, well, perhaps we'll find one lying about on the beach that nobody is using. 'Never lift your foot till you come to the stile'" (p. 93).

Obviously the Doctor is not one to tear his hair over problems of practical necessity (as we have already noted in his view of money). His attitude transcends the merely blithe, however; it is obvious that in many important respects, the Doctor is as much a child as Gub-Gub—though more charmingly so. His innocence is as attractive as his capacity to take pleasure in such small things as his boots. "'They really are splendid,' added the Doctor, gazing down at his feet with great satisfaction" (*Voyages*, p. 39). This anticipates the similar delight experienced by a "real" child, Ramona Quimby. In *Ramona the Pest* (1968), when she gets new boots, "beautiful red boots, *girl's* boots [she's been wearing a neighbor boy's hand-me-downs] . . . [Ramona] was . . . filled with joy" (p. 111).

Even more attractive are the Doctor's childishly insatiable curiosity about the new things which the natural world continuously offers him and his innocent openness to delight. "For many folks it would have seemed a creepy, nightmary sort of country, this land of the mangrove swamps. *But to the Doctor, for whom any kind of animal life was always companionable and good intentioned, it was a most delightful new field of exploration*" (emphasis added, *Post Office*, p. 321).

Not surprisingly, then, to many of the adults he meets the Doctor is either "ridiculous," as his sister has called him, or childish ("You'll never grow up, John," charges Sir William Peabody in *Circus*, p. 188). It is the satisfying incongruity and lovely irony of the Dolittle books that it is not the "wise" adults who understand the character and stature of the Doctor; it is, instead, the "dumb" animals to whom the Doctor is always "the great man." Their attitude toward him is often one of almost hushed veneration, not unlike that of Mole and Water Rat regarding Pan in the "Piper at the Gates of Dawn" chapter in *The Wind in the Willows*.

And why shouldn't it be? As the lioness in *Story* observes, "All the animals from here to the Indian Ocean are talking about this wonderful man, and how he can cure any kind of sickness, and how kind he is—the only man in the whole world who can talk the language of the animals!" (p. 72).

Not only does the doctor lovingly heal the animals' ills, but he also takes them seriously as individuals.

Just as Lofting took his young readers seriously. It is this attitude that, indeed, is an important reason the Dolittle books, published for the most part in the 1920s, are such groundbreaking works. He never wrote down to children. On the contrary. "What the intelligent child likes," he said, "is being written up to."

According to his biographer, Edward Blishen, "He detested the phrase 'a book for juveniles.' It was as absurd, he said . . . as to describe [an adult] book as being for 'seniles.'"[12] (Author-illustrator Robert Lawson would echo this sentiment in his 1941 Caldecott Medal acceptance speech: "There is something in that term 'Children's Illustrator' that seems to me slightly condescending to children. I think that if we are to make any distinction, we should speak of illustrators who work exclusively for adults as 'adult illustrators' and should say it with a slight curl of the lip."[13]

If Lofting has a fault as a writer, it may be a product of his respect for his young readers and an overestimation of their capacity for patience. There is a reason, alas, that many of the Dolittle books approach four hundred pages in length: It is that Lofting, as an author, never met a digression he didn't like! A classic example of what I mean occurs about midway through *Doctor Dolittle's Post Office*, when the Doctor decides to start a magazine for the animals, to be delivered worldwide by the newly created swallow mail. Nothing will do but that the narrative must then be interrupted for seven long chapters in which the animals (and the Doctor) swap stories to determine which should be published! To be sure, the stories are all charming and funny, but by today's editorial standards their inclusion seems self-indulgent and certainly disruptive of the plot's advance. Children are great natural editors, however, and I presume that many will do what I did as a child: simply skip the digressions and come back to them later, as time and interest permit. Indeed, successive generations of children *have* come back to the Dolittle books, delighted by their enduring powers of invention, their memorable characters, and the humor that so enlivens the experience of reading these modern classics.

Notes

[1] Eyre, Frank, *British Children's Books in the Twentieth Century*. New York: E. P. Dutton & Co., 1971, p. 65.

[2] Blishen, Edward, *Hugh Lofting (Three Bodley Head Monographs)*. London: The Bodley Head, 1968, p. 16.

[3] Blishen, p. 18.

[4] Blishen, p. 16.

[5] Townsend, John Rowe, *Written for Children* (3rd rev. ed.). New York: J. B. Lippincott, 1987, p. 147.

[6] Suhl, Isabelle, "The 'Real' Doctor Dolittle," in *The Black American in Books for Children: Readings in Racism* (2nd ed.). Metuchen, N.J.: The Scarecrow Press, Inc., 1985, p. 151.

[7] Lofting, Christopher, "Afterword," in *The Voyages of Doctor Dolittle* by Hugh Lofting (The Centenary Edition). New York: Delacorte Press, 1988, p. 314.

[8] Townsend, p. 149.

[9] Blishen, p. 12.

[10] Blishen, p. 10.

[11] Fisher, Margery, *Who's Who in Children's Books*. New York: Holt, Rinehart and Winston, 1975, p. 88.

[12] Blishen, pp. 14–15.

[13] Lawson, Robert, "Acceptance Paper," in *Caldecott Medal Books: 1938–1957*. Boston: The Horn Book, Inc., 1957, p. 66.

Chapter Three

MORE ABOUT ANIMALS AND OTHERS

"Well, pickle me and preserve me, if it isn't the talking pig."
—Freddy's Cousin Weedly *by Walter R. Brooks*

Seven years after the publication of *The Story of Doctor Dolittle*, the first book of a second author who shared both Lofting's respect for children *and* his talent to amuse appeared. The book was *To and Again* (1927) and the author was Walter R. Brooks, who once wrote:

"There is another question which has always bothered me. 'Why did you start writing books for children?' The answer is: I didn't. I wrote *To and Again* . . . for my own entertainment—that is, I wrote it in the way that got the most fun out of it for me. I used the same language in telling the story that I would have used in telling it to grownups. Why not? Children are people—they're just smaller and less experienced. They are not taken in by the smug playfulness of those who write or talk down to them as if they were dull-witted and slightly deaf."[1]

Brooks might be surprised by the prescience of his remarks. For his children's books are today celebrated by an international fan club, The Friends of Freddy, whose members are mostly adults who "reread with pleasure" Brooks's wonderful animal fantasies starring one of the great fictional animal characters in children's literature: Freddy the Pig.

This multigenerational popularity was equally true during the heyday of the Freddy series. Phyllis Fenner noted thirty-five years ago, "Yes, the *Freddy* books are to be reckoned with. . . . They are loved by all ages, from the littlest ones in school to those in Junior High. . . . Parents tell me they don't mind reading them aloud because they enjoy them so much themselves. . . . There is quite a bit of satire which parents get as they read. That is why, I suppose, older people and older children enjoy them as much as the littlest ones."[2]

In addition to their salutary respect for the intelligence of their juvenile readership, the Dolittle and Freddy books were groundbreaking events because they bucked the publishing trends of the 1920s. In *My Roads to Childhood*, published in 1939, Anne Carroll Moore assembled a 27-page list of "representative . . . books published [for children] 1926–1938."[3] Of her total of 134 titles listed, 31 were published in the 1920s. Of that 31, only one, *To and Again*—the first Freddy book—could accurately be described as humorous (none of the Dolittle series made the magisterial Miss Moore's list!). Two others—the memorable *Millions of Cats* by Wanda Gág and the now-forgotten *The Pigtail of Ah Lee Ben Loo* by John Bennett—might be described as whimsical. The balance of the titles, serious and sober-minded, can be loosely grouped in the following categories: American editions of foreign titles, realistic stories about foreign children, historical novels, the occasional boy's adventure story, and often didactic non-fiction.

A third reason why the Freddy books, especially, were ground-breaking, pathfinding, and generally innovative was their brisk use of the vernacular. To a lesser degree the Dolittle books do this as well, especially in the salty language of Polynesia the parrot and the genial illiteracies of Matthew Muggs, the Cat's-meat-Man, but Lofting's narrative voice is, at times, annoyingly old-fashioned to a modern reader's ears, especially in its use of "literary" inversions. ("This it was that had given it its name, the Amphitheatre," "To Mr. Bellamy's amusement park the citizens of Manchester came out in thousands," "And very gay and pretty it looked," etc. [all examples are from *Circus*] pp. 321–22.) As the satirist said of the early *Time* magazine: "Backward ran the sentences till reeled the mind."

Brooks's narrative voice, on the other hand, was as simple, un-adorned, and *natural* as his dialogue. He was doing for children's literature what the Down East humorists of the 1830s had done for American literature for adults. And like them, he was criticized for his innovative style: One librarian huffed, "Slang of the comic strip type and bad grammar are frequently found in the conversational parts. Libraries can do without [*Freddy the Detective*, 1932]."[4] Happily, others were more perceptive. Anne Carroll Moore herself allowed that she was ". . . impressed by the ease and naturalness of Mr. Brooks's writing. . . ."[5] The natural-ness and the contemporaneity of Brooks's language help make his books as attractive and accessible today as when they were first published decades ago.

Both Lofting and Brooks wrote series books. There were twelve Doctor Dolittle books, and more than twice that number (twenty-five in all) chronicled Freddy's adventures. (It's interesting that so many enormously popular series for children are humorous in tone—perhaps this is a reason that critics have so undervalued the literary worth of the series as a form!)

Though both Lofting and Brooks wrote animal fantasies, their works differ in one fundamental aspect: The hero of Lofting's work is a human being who, though he is often helped by the animals, just as often helps them. Indeed, it is the Doctor who is the innovator, the catalyst for action; it is he who starts the birds' post office, for example, and it is he, not the animals, who manages it. In contrast, it is the animals of the Bean Farm who control the action in the Freddy books, and it is one of their number, Freddy, who is the undisputed star: Freddy, that multifaceted, multitalented pig of many parts—poet, politician, pilot, pied piper, publisher, detective, banker, cowboy, and more.

However diverse Freddy's roles, though, his adventures had at least two things in common, both of which are neatly summarized by his publisher, Alfred Knopf, on the dust jacket of Freddy's sixth adventure, *Wiggins for President*: The books, Knopf noted, were "All by Walter Brooks," and they were "All Funny."

In fact, the series as a whole deftly demonstrates the diversity of what most of the theorists we met in chapter one agree is funny. If the series has traditionally been undervalued and neglected by the critics, that is surely not Freddy's (or Brooks's) fault but is instead due to the fact that, as E. B. White has noted, humor is usually relegated to the cheap seats at the back of the critical house. "The world likes humor," White observed, "but it treats it patronizingly. It decorates its serious artists with laurel, and its wags with Brussels sprouts."[6] To reread the Freddy books (now, sadly, all out of print) is to realize the inequity of this, for Freddy and his Bean Farm cronies, though they made their first appearance almost seventy years ago, continue to command the gift of laughter.

Like many other humorists, Walter R. Brooks was a man of serious demeanor. "I'm not continually trying to be funny, thank goodness!" he testily told a reporter in 1938. "My fun is confined to my writing."[7]

In addition to the Freddy books, that writing included one comic novel for adults, *Ernestine Takes Over* (Morrow, 1935), the rather bawdy humor of which was often compared to that of Thorne "Topper" Smith; a guidebook to New York City (*New York, An Intimate Guide*, Knopf, 1931); and some two hundred short stories for adult readers. Twenty-seven of that total starred another talking-animal hero, a horse named Ed, the inspiration for the popular 1960s television series *Mr. Ed*.

Brooks often claimed that his "short stories in the adult magazines are really nothing but children's stories, changed a little. There's no difference in the method, just in the things you refer to."[8] What he most often referred to in the adult short stories was the battle between the sexes, the war between (married) men and women. He viewed this connubial contest from a satiric remove, and the stories he concocted about it have the brittle, wisecracking, sophisticated, and occasionally zany tone of the screwball comedies of 1930s movies and may, in fact, have influenced them.

The only time he addressed this issue in a Freddy book—at least in human terms—was in *Freddy's Cousin Weedly* (1940), where we meet Mr. Bean's aunt Effie and her husband, Lucius Snedeker. "Uncle Snedeker," Brooks writes cheerfully, "was usually considered to be a pretty good husband. That is, he almost always did what Aunt Effie told him to . . ." (p. 90). Lofting's attitude toward marriage (or at least his appreciation of its satiric possibilities) is similar to Brooks's. The worst threat that Dr.

Dolittle's sister, Sarah, can offer him is: "If you don't send [an alligator that is eating the linoleum] away this minute I'll—I'll go and get married!" The Doctor's reply seems to suggest the dire nature of this threat and the union it contemplates: "All right," he says, "go and get married. *It can't be helped*" (emphasis added, *The Story of Doctor Dolittle*, pp. 22–23). In a scenario Brooks would have appreciated, Lofting further posits an island society in the Pacific Ocean where the husbands lived on one island and the wives on the other. "Sensible people, some of them savages," Matthew Muggs comments dryly (*The Voyages of Doctor Dolittle*, p. 11).

In the wars fought in the Freddy books between the animals and their human adversaries, the usual motivation is not sexual one-upmanship but personal gain, instead. If money is a nuisance to Dr. Dolittle, it is a passion for such villains as Herb Garble, Aaron Doty, and Mr. EHA, villains who provide the plot-driving conflict in many of the Freddy books.

The tone of the books is different from the short stories, as well; though witty and often satiric, the books are gentler and sweeter, and in the variety of their comic invention they are more enduringly satisfying. The laughter in Freddy is engendered not only by situation and wisecracks but by devices and concerns that have informed the whole history of humorous writing. As critic Sheila Egoff notes, "[The Freddy books] are, indeed, in the classic humorous mold: the stories begin with order, move to disorder, and revert to order."[9]

The disorder that sets the whole comic machinery in motion usually derives from a character quirk or defect—often pride or greed—and must be dealt with if order is to be restored to the idyllic life of Bean Farm and the nearby village of Centerboro. The Freddy books are quintessential agrarian/small-town idyll, and the problems that threaten their order often reflect the loss of innocence and the advent of urban disorder that the Industrial Revolution visited on American life in the last century.

If Lofting's life was ambiguously international, Brooks's was inarguably American: He was born in 1886 (on January 9, just five days before Lofting was born) in the small and peaceful upstate New York town of Rome. As an adult he moved to the Big City (New York), where he found (modest) fame and fortune, moving back to another small town, Roxbury, New York, where he spent the last ten years of his life (order, disorder, order).

Brooks's family were Yankees, emigrating from Vermont and Massachusetts to upstate New York around the end of the eighteenth century. His maternal and paternal grandfathers were born in 1805 and 1821, respectively. And since Brooks lived until 1958, his life and that of his immediate family spanned a century and a half of American life. Most notably Brooks's own formative years were spent before the turn of the century.

In this brief biographical context, it makes perfect sense that machines, a product of the Industrial Revolution, should be an object of mistrust and humor in the Freddy books. Mr. and Mrs. Bean, Freddy's owners, do not have an automobile, for example, but travel by horse and buggy instead. Other characters do own automobiles, but America's favorite machine is usually unreliable at best when it does make an appearance.

"But who is this who approaches at such reckless speed?" the eagle Breckenridge exclaims. "Ah, the estimable sheriff."

"Hop in," the sheriff tells Freddy as they start off in his automobile in pursuit of the villainous Mr. Winch. "Hold on tight" (*Freddy and Mr. Camphor*, 1944, p. 196).

This, of course, is delicious—and funny—irony, for the reader already knows that the sheriff's car is so ancient and slow that it might attain the "reckless" speed of fifteen miles per hour—going downhill with a brisk tail wind. (Dr. Dolittle would probably have been intrigued by automobiles or other modern machinery, but since the implied historical setting of the Lofting books is pre–Industrial Revolution, this consideration is never brought into comedic play.)

In this same mildly Luddite context we have Mr. Bean's uncle Ben, an inventor and mechanic whose work is brilliant but . . . flawed. Consider his invention of an alarm clock that shoots off a series of firecrackers but explodes the clock in the process! Or his work as a mechanic, which can best be described as serendipitous:

". . . for when he had fixed an article, it often seemed to have turned into something entirely different. Like the time Mrs. Bean's washing machine broke down, and he fixed it, and afterwards, it wouldn't wash anymore, and when you turned it on, it got very hot, so they used it as an oven to keep Mr. Bean's supper warm when he was late" (*Freddy the Pilot*, 1952, p. 61).

It is probably not too surprising that, in due course, Uncle Ben invents an automobile engine, "The Benjamin Bean Atomic Engine," with predictable results:

"So [Freddy and his friend Jinx, the cat] got into the station wagon and hung on tight to their seats. And Uncle Ben started the engine. . . . It had so much power that when it started . . . you had to have a good grip on the seats or you were likely to be left behind. It almost seemed to gather its wheels under it and jump. . . . In three seconds it was out of the gate and streaking up the road.

"Back on the porch Mrs. Bean smiled placidly. 'I do like to see our animals having so much fun.'

"'By cracky,' said Mr. Bean, 'if ridin' with Uncle Ben's fun, I guess I'd as soon be sick abed!'" (*Freddy and the Men from Mars*, 1954, pp. 13–14).

In a series where greed for personal gain is a reliable motive for villainy, it is no surprise that those—like bankers—who possess and control money should be the object of both the villains' schemes and Brooks's good-natured humor.

Freddy himself is a banker, although "for a poet to be president of the [First Animal] bank had always seemed to [Freddy] something of a joke" (*Freddy and the Ignormus*, 1941, p. 95). (Technically it's not a joke but an exercise in incongruity.) But it is the human banker, Mr. Weezer, President of the First National Bank of Centerboro, who is the more reliable source of laughter.

This is sometimes the product of physical humor (he gets his head caught under a theater seat while looking for a lost coin and has to be pulled out by the heels in *Freddy the Magician*, 1947) but is more often the by-product of a running gag that recurs throughout the series: His glasses jump off his nose whenever a sum larger than five dollars is mentioned (ten dollars in later books—one of the few instances of the inflationary exigencies of the real world intruding).

Having established this gag, Brooks pulls a neat twist on it in *Wiggins*. Freddy, disguised as an old Irishwoman, Mrs. O'Halloran, is coerced into depositing his life's savings in the First National Bank of Centerboro.

"And how large a sum is it?" Mr. Weezer asks, anticipating a large amount of capital.

"Freddy looked in the shopping bag. 'Eighteen cents,' he said.

"And for the first and only time in his life Mr. Weezer's glasses fell off at the mention of a sum under ten dollars!" (p. 222).

Although Freddy's adversary in his first appearance in the series—he is afraid Freddy's foray into banking will drive the humans' bank out of business—Mr. Weezer becomes one of Freddy's staunchest friends and sagest advisers in later books.

Other wealthy people who are equally sympathetic—but eccentric, recalling Gub-Gub's remark—are Mrs. Church and Mr. C. Jimson Camphor (a whole chapter could be devoted to the comic names in the Freddy books).

Mrs. Church wears dime-store jewelry ("Why wear diamonds when you can get the same effect with glass at a fraction of the cost?" [*Freddy and the Popinjay*, 1945, p. 32]), while Mr. Camphor, concerned that he is too frivolous to command credibility in business dealings, hires a butler, Bannister, to provide dignity on demand.

In addition to the mechanical and the mercenary, Brooks loved lampooning authority as well, especially the elected variety. In so doing, he was operating within the framework of a long American tradition, for if there was a recognizably American humor by 1830, as Walter Blair claims,[10] politicians were being lampooned and lambasted almost from its beginnings—or at least as early as the publication of Seba Smith's "Jack Downing" letters in 1833.

Pity the poor politician who wanders into Brooks's pages, where he is invariably depicted as self-importantly ineffectual (Senator Blunder in *Freddy and the Bean Home News*, 1943), scheming (the Washington, D.C., woodpeckers in *Wiggins*), or pompous and long-winded: When the animals go to Florida on vacation in the very first of the Freddy books, they stop off in the nation's capital, where their senator greets them by (what else?) making a speech:

"To welcome a delegation of the home folks . . . is one of the few pleasures that cheer the burdened brow of those whose stern duty it is to keep their shoulder always to the wheel of the ship of State. And that reminds me of the story of the two Irishmen . . ." (*To and Again*, p. 57).

Constance Rourke points out, in her landmark work *American Humor: A Study of the National Character*, "The American people relished oratory. With the beginnings of Jacksonian democracy public speech burst forth in a never-ending flood."[11] Brooks may have ridden the crest of that flood as a boy, for both his maternal grandfather and his uncle were early mayors of Rome and political powerhouses in the Democratic Party, both locally and nationally (both men were also bank presidents). Or perhaps it was simply that he was himself a good Yankee who valued and celebrated the virtues of thoughtful silence and taciturnity, notably in the characters of Mr. Bean and Uncle Ben. (His admiration for economy of words does not prevent him from satirizing even this, when Uncle Ben and General Grimm ["famous throughout the whole army for saying as few words as possible in as loud a voice as possible . . ."] have what can best be described as a "silence contest" [*Freddy the Pilot*, p. 68].)

If silence is golden grist for Brooks's humor mill, what about the opposite—logorrhea? Consider that inveterate talker, Charles the rooster:

"Like most people who love to make speeches, he could talk for hours on any subject, whether he knew anything about it or not, and the things he said sounded fine until you thought about them, and then you realized that they didn't mean much of anything" (*Ignormus*, p. 48).

Like Lofting, Brooks loved playing with language. Its use and misuse and antic wordplay are a regular and consistent source of the Freddy books' best humor.

True to the time and place of his upbringing and operating in an American humorous tradition dating back to the 1830s, Brooks loved inventing comic and archaic-sounding exclamations and regionalisms. Brooks was a Yankee, as already noted, and

Constance Rourke records that "the Yankee had created a speech of his own with an abundance of homely metaphor; and his lingo was greatly relished even outside of New England. 'Coming on full chisel.' 'Saw my old hat in two if I don't do it.'" Such expressions, she notes, "were garnered in almanacs and joke books that penetrated to all parts of the country."[12] Though he never commented on the fact, Brooks must have been aware of and relished this tradition, gleefully creating new examples of "homely metaphor" and "Yankee lingo."

Uncle Snedeker, whom we have already met, is a rich source of these: "Well, set fire to my coat tails!" "Well, perfume my handkerchief!" "Well, pickle me and preserve me if it isn't the talking pig!" And "Well, tear off my collar and necktie!" To which Aunt Effie tartly retorts, "I will *not* have this dreadful swearing, Snedeker . . ." (*Weedly*, p. 146).

Freddy's friend Leo the lion is another reliable source: "Well, dye my hair!" (*Freddy and the Perilous Adventure*, 1942, p. 130), "Well, fry me in butter!" (*Freddy the Pied Piper*, 1946, p. 213), while "Great potatoes!" is Sheriff Higgins's contribution (*Weedly*, p. 108). One of Freddy's human friends, the sheriff also gives Brooks a splendid opportunity to satirize the language of the law:

"The Sheriff had found that the language of the law is pretty terrifying to guilty people, and so in cases like this he always used it. But there is one great trouble with the language of the law. The sentences are so long that very few people except judges can get through them without stopping to take a breath in the middle. And, of course, this spoils their impressiveness. So in his last sentence the Sheriff had not stopped but had used up all his breath right down to the bottom of his lungs, with the result that he was unable to conclude, as he should, by glaring sternly at the culprits. He merely sank down in a chair, whooping and gulping to get his breathing started again" (*Freddy and Mr. Camphor*, pp. 192–93).

Another rich source of such semantic satire is eagles, who, "since they are the national bird, have a great sense of their own dignity, and feel that just ordinary talk is beneath them . . ." (*Perilous Adventure*, p. 52).

We have already met Breckenridge wondering "who is this who approaches at such reckless speed?" Here he is again, this time unexpectedly encountering Freddy, who is now aloft in a hot-air balloon (don't ask how he got there): "Welcome, oh pig, to the starry upper spaces of the blue empyrean" (p. 52).

No simple "hello" here.

Language is not always used for satiric purposes in the Freddy books—or in the Dolittle books, for that matter. Sometimes it defines character. Breckenridge the eagle and Charles the rooster from the Freddy books are good examples of this. Polynesia the parrot is an equally good example from the Dolittle series. Her speech, at turns sarcastic, caustic, and—given her age and experience of the world—self-importantly didactic, tells us everything we need to know about her. (And if we had any doubts about her early life as a sailor, there is her swearing—dreadful enough to give Aunt Effie an attack of the vapors. . . .)

Sometimes language is simply a playful end in itself. Consider Ollie Groper from the Freddy books; the man is both the proprietor of the Centerboro Hotel *and* a walking dictionary:

"I've always had a predilection for this here sesquipedalianism. I mean . . . big words. They were kind of a hobby. Which it is bad. It habituates you to imperspicuity" (*Magician*, p. 168).

Indeed!

Or consider Mr. Condiment, the villainous comic-book publisher of *Freddy the Pilot* who is less walking dictionary than traveling thesaurus:

"Put in a line of Condiment Comics and from the minute you open in the morning, the place'll be jammed, teeming, populous—I mean to say, crowded" (p. 81).

The joyful exuberance of words arguably reaches its apotheosis in the character of Mr. Boomschmidt, Freddy's friend, owner of Boomschmidt's Colossal and Unparalleled Circus, and a great comic creation.

To the uninitiate, Mr. Boom may seem to be only a perpetually bewildered little fat man in a brightly checked suit. In fact he is a shrewd manager of people and averter of crises. His straight "man" is always Freddy's friend Leo the lion.

Consider this scene from *Pilot*. Mr. Boom speaks:

"'We ran into a little trouble on our way north. . . . I wonder what the word for it is? Leo, what would the word for it be?'

"'Word for what, Chief?'

"'What we're in.'

"'Dilemma,' said the lion. 'That's what you said last night.'

"'Gracious!' said Mr. Boomschmidt. 'Sounds awful, doesn't it? What's it mean?'

"'It's your word, not mine,' said Leo.

"Mr. Bean took the pipe out of his mouth. 'Same as a quandary,' he said and put the pipe back.

"'A quandary,' said Mr. Boomschmidt thoughtfully. 'Ah, yes, quite right—a quandary. Well, Leo . . .'

"'It's a bird, I think, Chief,' said the lion. 'Kind of a cross between a swan and a cassowary. Lives in Africa. My Uncle Ajax used to tell me stories about the flocks of wild quandaries on Lake Nyasa—'" (pp. 11–12).

The quandary is the product of the evil Mr. Condiment's quest to marry the circus's equestrienne, Mademoiselle Rose. To that end he sends his attorney, Mr. Newsome, to stop the show:

"'Funny name, Gizling,' Mr. Boomschmidt said. 'But so's Boomschmidt, for that matter. Newsome now—that's a nice name. Too bad it's so like Nuisance though. Must make you very sad when you think of it.'

"'My client,' said Mr. Newsome, 'feels that he has been very patient with Mademoiselle Rose and with you. But he has reached the end of his patience. He wishes me to warn you that if within three days Mademoiselle Rose does not agree to marry him, he intends to take much more drastic measures.'

"'Drastic, drastic?' said Mr. Boomschmidt thoughtfully. 'I'm afraid I don't know what kind of a measure that is. You see, I just learned in school the ordinary measures, like four cups one pint, two pints one gallon, and so on. . . .'

"Nobody could talk to Mr. Boomschmidt and keep his temper if Mr. Boomschmidt wanted him to lose it. Mr. Newsome lost his completely at this point. He turned very red and jumped up and down with anger. 'If you'll just *let* me, I wish to *tell* you what Mr. Condiment *said*,' he yelled.

"'Oh, does Mr. Condiment know about miles and inches?' Mr. Boomschmidt asked mildly. 'Well, that's very kind of him to help us out, but as I told you, I have it all down in a little book, and—'

"'A-a-ach!' said Mr. Newsome disgustedly, and he turned around and started for the gate" (pp. 157–59).

Though generally too gentle for its extended treatment, the books occasionally feature another kind of verbal humor—sarcasm—as well, usually through the speech of the two owls, Old Whibley and Uncle Solomon, the screech owl.

In *Freddy and the Bean Home News* our hero goes to Whibley's home in the woods to ask for advice (for reasons too complicated to explain here, Freddy is disguised as a little boy wearing a sailor suit that belonged to Mr. Bean when *he* was a boy):

"He had to rap several times before the owl's head finally appeared in the hole high up in the trunk.

"'Well, what is it?' he said testily. 'Don't knock the tree down.'

"'It's me, Freddy,' said the pig.

"'Of course it's you,' said Old Whibley. 'Nobody else would be silly enough to put on a sailor suit for a walk in the woods. Or have you come to invite me to go for a sail in your yacht?'

"'It's a disguise,' said Freddy.

"'Very poor one,' said the owl. 'Fifty years behind the style. Disguise should be right up to the minute in style. Then nobody notices you. The more stylish you are, the more you're like everybody else, and the less attention you attract. Besides which, you look foolish in that suit.'

"'I suppose you're right,' said Freddy. 'But I wanted to ask your advice.'

"'Of course you do. Never see you unless you want help'" (p. 147).

Brooks softens the sarcasm by demonstrating that the owls are genuinely fond of Freddy and often serve as his attorneys when he has been falsely accused of a crime (which happens about once per book) and is in danger of going to jail. In fact, Freddy and Doctor Dolittle probably spend more time in prison than any other characters in modern children's literature. Freddy's incarcerations are usually more pleasant than the Doctor's, however, since they are spent in the Centerboro jail. Centerboro, of course, is so idyllic that it has no crime, and therefore the sheriff must keep "a nice comfortable jail that people want to stay in . . . so now and then they break a few unimportant laws so they can get sent there . . ." (*Weedly*, pp. 25–26). Once there, the prisoners don't want to leave, just as many of the animals who come to Doctor Dolitte's house for treatment find *it* so idyllic that they don't wish to leave either.

Whether Freddy always winds up in jail or not, it is usually not so much his freedom that is in jeopardy but his dignity. For Freddy, like Gub-Gub, is given to occasional pomposity and vanity, always cues for Brooks (and Lofting, too) to employ some form of slapstick or physical humor to bring Freddy or Gub-Gub back to earth—literally, in Freddy's case, when he falls into the odd thornbush or rain barrel. Brooks is especially good at this and demonstrates a mastery of building comic suspense in *Wiggins*, where, as previously noted, it takes him fourteen pages to get Freddy onto a bicycle so that he can immediately fall off. Part of the excitement of this type of humorous suspense is the anticipation that informs it, for the reader knows Freddy's tumble is inevitable; when it finally comes, we laugh as much in relief and vindication as in delight.

Freddy is not the only one whose vanity is assaulted, however. Jinx the cat falls into a pond when he leans over too far to admire his reflection. And Leo the lion nearly ruins the animals' escape from jeopardy (in *Pied Piper*) when he insists on stopping to wash out his mane ("And I ought to have another permanent; there isn't hardly a crinkle left in the darn thing . . ." [p.92]).

Brooks's treatment of Leo demonstrates the subtle difference that occasionally manifests itself in the way Brooks and Lofting portray animal characters. Lofting, as previously noted, presented his characters as true to their essential animal natures and to our traditional beliefs about their natures (not always the same, of course). Brooks does this too, in most cases (for example, Jinx is a cat through and through; and the dogs Robert and Georgie are as doglike as Jip—but without an English accent!). Leo, however, is an exercise in incongruity. His passion for permanent waves and for having his claws manicured are neither realistic lion traits nor manifestations of traditional beliefs about the behavior of the king of the beasts, but when contrasted with these latter two, Leo's quirks become incongruously funny. Moreover, because Leo is true to the character Brooks has created for him, on the rare occasions when he isn't, when he *does* manifest realistic lion behavior, he becomes an even more comic figure—when, for example, he demonstrates for Freddy how he plans to deal with a villainous character. He glares ferociously at Freddy with his yellow lion's eyes, and Freddy is also no longer the literary Freddy but, instead, a pig facing a lion. "Hey, quit that!" Freddy says nervously. "I—I don't like it." Leo ignores him and continues to stare, and then, without warning, suddenly twitches his whiskers, and Freddy "jumped convulsively backward and fell over a chair" (*Pied Piper*, p. 104). Afterward he explains sheepishly to Leo that he sometimes forgets his friend is a lion. So does the reader.

A more dramatic demonstration of the occasional difference between Lofting and Brooks is their treatment of a fox hunt. Both deplore the "sport," viewing it, as Oscar Wilde so famously did, as "the unspeakable in pursuit of the inedible." Lofting, however, to dramatize his distaste, presents the foxes as being essentially helpless victims who would have been swiftly—and horribly—destroyed by the hounds and the hunters if the Doctor had not been there to intervene. To prevent future potentially fatal encounters of fox and hounds, the Doctor gives the vixen bottles of camphor and eucalyptus to confound the hounds' sense of smell (*Doctor Dolittle's Circus*). Brooks, on the other hand, gives us an intelligent, self-sufficient fox who, without human intervention, is able to outwit both hounds and hunters on his own. "But pshaw, Freddy," John the fox says, "you don't need to worry about me, though it's nice that you do. But if I can't fool a pack of silly hounds, I deserve to get chewed up" (*Freddy Rides Again*, 1951, p. 31).

How John does fool the hounds is partly realism (Brooks was a talented amateur naturalist) and partly invention, but both parts are invested with foxily sly humor, and John emerges as both a believable animal and an exercise in acceptable anthropomorphism.

Lofting's is the bleaker view, not surprisingly, since his view of humankind was far bleaker than was Brooks's. But when it comes to animal characters, both writers are similar in the spirit of celebration they bring to their depictions. And in this regard, too, the humor of both series is rooted in delight—in the delight both of discovery and, yes, of predictable familiarity. A wonderful air of benign, good-humored geniality informs the best books in both series. What Sheila Egoff has written of the Freddy books, "[They] shine with the joy of being alive," can be said with equal vigor of the Dolittle books.[13]

And it is this glow that may be their most enlightening and enduring contribution to children's literature.

Notes

[1] "Walter R. Brooks," Knopf promotional brochure, n.d. (ca. 1945), p. 4.

[2] Fenner, Phyllis, *The Proof of the Pudding*. New York: The John Day Company, 1957, p. 66.

[3] Moore, Anne Carroll, *My Roads to Childhood*. New York: Doubleday, Doran & Company, Inc., 1939, pp. 339 et seq.

[4] King, Jessica, "Freddy the Detective" (Review). *Library Journal* 57:865 (October 15, 1932).

[5] Moore, Anne Carroll, "The Three Owls' Notebook." *The Horn Book* XXV:116 (March/April 1949).

[6] White, E. B., and Katharine S. White, eds., *A Subtreasury of American Humor*. New York: The Modern Library, 1941, p. xviii.

[7] "Two Authors," *Utica Observer Dispatch*, February 1, 1938, p. 12.

[8] "On an Author," *New York Herald Tribune Book Review*. November 15, 1953, p. 2.

[9] Egoff, Sheila A., *Worlds Within*. Chicago: American Library Association, 1988, p. 127.

[10] Blair, Walter, *Native American Humor (1800–1900)*. New York: American Book Company, 1937, p. 3.

[11] Rourke, Constance, *American Humor: A Study of the National Character*. New York: Harcourt, Brace and Company, 1931, p. 63.

[12] Rourke, p. 28.

[13] Egoff, p. 127.

Chapter Four

THE OTHERS

"I have a terrible dread that we shall take our children's books too seriously and solemnly."
—*Robert Lawson, Caldecott Medal Acceptance Speech, 1941*

No Man Is a Hero . . . to His Pet

The seldom solemn author-illustrator Robert Lawson was born in New York City on October 4, 1892, but grew up in the New Jersey suburb of Montclair, living for a time in a house once owned by the artist George Innes. In fact, according to Sue Lile Inman, "He and his brother shared a spacious, well-lit room that had been Innes's studio."[1] If this was a significant influence on his decision to become an artist, it was a long time in manifesting itself. As his wife, Marie A. Lawson, recalls, "[As a child] he neither drew pictures nor wrote stories, as many children do. It was not until high school days . . . that he produced his first drawing."[2] The drawing earned him first place in a poster contest, and the dollar prize was the first dollar he ever earned.

That fact seems to have had about as much influence on his decision to go to art school as living in Innes's studio had. His three years of study (1911–1914) at New York's School of Fine and Applied Arts were "more of a trial than the definite adoption of a profession" (again according to Marie). World War I commanded his military service in France, where he did camouflage work at the front. Returning to New York after the war, he launched a career as a commercial artist.

"The ten years which followed were wholly commercial years. But they have never been regretted, for the very limitations and requirements imposed brought a greater technical versatility, the necessary limits of space, a finer sense of design; the rendering of actual products, a more accurate observance of detail, a finer draughtsmanship."[3]

These same skills became hallmarks of his later work as an illustrator of children's books, of course. But there was another element that informed his early work and that would prove even more significant later: his fondness for introducing an element of the fantastic into even the most realistic picture, what Marie called "that something else . . . the tiny figure of a young knight before a medieval castle, a Centaur ruthlessly trampling the neat borders of a New England garden; even before the high towers of modern Manhattan elves lurk in the remaining shrubbery."[4]

(Interestingly enough, Walter R. Brooks was doing the same thing with words in his early stories for adults published in the 1920s and early 1930s: Pan appears in Central Park, unicorns lurk at the bottom of suburban gardens, nymphs dwell in the copse at the property line. Perhaps both men were trying to recapture the childhood time "when," as Robert Lawson wrote in his memoir *At That Time*, "we were blissfully unconscious of any dividing line between fact and fancy; a happy if muddleheaded period before the laws of the grown-up world made a definite cleavage between what we imagined and what was real."[5])

In any event Lawson's love for drawing "leprechauns, giants, dragons, and other fantastic beings"[6] was recognized by the great children's book editor May Massee and was rewarded with his first commission to illustrate a children's book: Arthur Mason's fanciful *The Wee Men of Ballywooden* (Doubleday, Doran, 1930). (Actually Lawson had illustrated a children's book as early as 1922: George R. Chester's *The Adventures of Little Prince Toofat* [McCann]. Now extremely rare, the book was disavowed by Lawson because he was unhappy with the quality of the reproduction of his illustrations. Accordingly the title does not appear in most bibliographies of his work.)

And so a new career was launched: children's book illustrator. During the decade of the 1930s he would illustrate twenty-eight books by other authors (nine in 1937 alone!).

The two most notable of these, *The Story of Ferdinand* (Viking, 1936) and *Mr. Popper's Penguins* (Little, Brown, 1938), demonstrate Lawson's affection for animals, his draughtsman's appreciation for their "animal symmetry," and his satirist's comprehension of their comic possibilities ("Like all fabulists he often used animals to comment on human actions"[7]).

Still others (*Betsy Ross, Francis Scott Key* [both Whittlesey, 1936], *Drums of Monmouth* [Dodd, Mead, 1935], *Haven's End* [Little, Brown, 1933], etc.) demonstrate his "other abiding interest . . . his country and its history."[8] In fact, his first published drawing, which appeared in the *Harper's Weekly* of January 30, 1915, was for a poem on the invasion of Belgium in World War I. (Coincidentally, Walter R. Brooks's first published work, an ode titled "Haunted," was published in *Century* magazine the same year). Lawson was, simply, a patriot at a time when, as Barbara Bader has pointed out, "it was still possible to be patriotic in this simple, open fashion without being smug."[9]

Put together Lawson's fondness for blurring the line between fact and fantasy, his comprehension of the comic possibilities of animals, and his abiding interest in his country and its history, and the nearly inevitable result is the first book that Lawson would write *and* illustrate, *Ben and Me* (1939), "a new and astonishing life of Benjamin Franklin as written by his good mouse Amos as its subtitle tells us."

The idea of writing the life of a great man as seen through the eyes of an animal had been suggested several years prior to the book's publication in 1939 by Lawson's editor at Little, Brown. And so, as Lawson reported in a 1941 speech, he "made a list of famous people and clawed it over and then I stewed over it for several weeks and then settled more or less on Ben Franklin. He'd always struck me as a pretty pompous, self-satisfied old scoundrel. . . ."[10] The fur cap Dr. Franklin always wore "and which I have always felt must have been inhabited by *something*"[11] provided a clue as to what kind of animal should be chosen as biographer, but it was a chance remark by Marie Lawson that provided the necessary "Eureka" of discovery: "That fur cap certainly is an awful looking rat's nest." "Well," Lawson recalled, "that was just what we needed. If it was a rat's nest, why not a mouses's? So Amos suddenly took form. The origin of the name is simple. Amos—A Mouse."[12]

The rest is history—of a sort. *Ben and Me* would be the first of four of what Lawson liked to call his "cock-eyed histories," "a sort of series giving the real lowdown on various historical characters." Joining Franklin in this gallery of slightly skewed portraits would be Christopher Columbus, Paul Revere, and Captain Kidd.

The basic humor of this comic quartet comes not in the use of animals as human surrogates but in the use of animals to record, with superiority, satire, and (occasionally) affection, the failings and foibles of human beings.

Lawson's approach to all four books was epitomized in what he wrote of *Captain Kidd's Cat* (1956): "In a book of this sort it is customary to clothe a skeleton of fairly well established facts with humor and imagination. . . ." The "clothing," in terms of the research Lawson did for the books, was carefully and elaborately realized. "In the past fifteen years," Lawson recorded, "I have done about fifteen books. *Captain Kidd's Cat* occupied slightly over a year; research, writing and illustrations, the latter alone taking over ten months of hard labor."[13]

As the series evolved, Lawson became more interested in history and less in humor. *Mr. Revere and I* (1953) and *Captain Kidd's Cat* offer much more richly realized historic settings and chronicles of historic fact than *Ben and Me* and *I Discover Columbus* (1941). In fact, while the first and the last are both revisionist histories, the former takes humorous exception to the accepted proprieties of the historic record by deflating the reputation of Dr. Franklin, while the latter is at pains to *restore* (perhaps even embellish) the reputation of Kidd and to depict him, not as bloodthirsty buccaneer, but as a respectable trader and honest merchant. The attitude of the animal "biographers" is, accordingly, quite different, for if Amos patronizes, McDermot (Capt. K's cat) admires; if Amos scorns, McDermot sanctifies. The reader may guess which of the two books is the more humorous. . . .

If there is less humor in the last two books, what remains is, nevertheless, rooted in the same incongruity that more richly informs the first two. Lawson establishes this in the Foreword to the very first book: "I am aware," he reports, "that [Amos's] account of Franklin's career differs in many respects from the accounts of later historians. This I cannot explain but it seems reasonable to believe that statements made by one who lived on terms of such intimacy with this great man should be more trustworthy than those written by later scholars."

Well . . . if it is true that no man is a hero to his valet, it is equally true that no man is a hero to his mouse! Consider the portrait of poor, hapless Franklin that Amos paints: "He was undeniably stupid at times" (p. 4). "He just looked . . . silly" (p. 8). "He was really very irritating" (p. 22). He's clumsy: When he steps back to admire his invention, he trips over his saw. When he swims, he "snorts and splashes like an overgrown grampus" (p. 24). He's vain: "Ben was just overenthusiastic about himself" (p. 18). He's scattered and distracted: "Ben never had his wits about him" (p. 20). He's hypocritical, forever spouting high-sounding maxims that he, himself, refuses to live by. He is, in short, a child. How does he celebrate the signing of the Declaration of Independence? By shooting off firecrackers, "and [he] was noisier than any of the youths. He managed to burn most of his fingers . . ." (p. 70).

And so Amos, the parent mouse, must take charge. He lectures ("In some ways, Ben, you're fairly bright . . ." [p. 15]) and he chastises: "I had to be rather sharp with him before he would settle down to food" (p. 15).

Ben, with his eagerly inquisitive scientific mind, which distracts him from the realities of the quotidian world, is a man-child like Doctor Dolittle, and, like the Doctor, he is blessed (and occasionally cursed, given their sometimes bossy natures) with animals who function as his surrogate parents—and as his friends. The difference lies in the animals' attitude toward their respective human charges. The Dolittle animals manage the realities of the Doctor's life for him out of respect, even veneration. Amos manages (or tries to manage) Ben's affairs out of sheer self-importance and exasperation. This could be tiresome if the reader didn't quickly realize that, in his way, Amos is as much a humbug as Franklin. The humor derives from the readers' pleasure in seeing BOTH egoes punctured. Amos may claim that "the only remarkable thing about the whole business was ME!" (p. 21), but he is routinely demonstrated to be not as smart as he thinks he is. Consider the *Poor Richard's Almanack* affair. Ben, though more or less retired from the printing business, still loves "to putter around among the presses, reading proofs and *getting in the way generally*" (emphasis added, p. 33). Amos likes to putter himself. But when he decides to "improve" the *Almanack* without telling Ben, the result is disaster:

"'Fly, Dr. Franklin! Fly for your life!' [the harbormaster] shouted" (p. 34). It seems that Amos has made "a few corrections in the Tide Table" where "it appeared wrong to me," and a mob of angry shipmasters whose vessels have run aground are en route to Ben's home with mayhem in mind.

Despite Amos's low opinion of Franklin, we see in this incident that he is, in fact, quick-witted and calm in adversity. He convinces the mob that the Almanack they have purchased is but "a scurrilous counterfeit of MY Almanack." (Amos has modestly replaced the name "Poor Richard" with his own wherever it appears. Franklin astutely points this out to the mob: "If you will but look with care at this scurrilous counterfeit of MY Almanack, you will find nowhere in it the name Poor Richard, but only that of one Amos, no doubt a contemptible, ignorant and inaccurate fellow" (pp. 36–37).

When the mollified mob has finally dispersed, Franklin, looking "very stern and solemn" says, "Amos, I smell a rat" (p. 38).

This incident also demonstrates Ben's kindness and generosity of spirit, for, as Amos admits, he "never thereafter mentioned my little adventure in printing." Lest the humor be compromised by sentiment, however, Amos is quick to add, "so I tried to be somewhat more lenient about his maxims . . . trying though they were . . ." (p. 39).

Maxims provide humor in the Freddy books as well, where they are tried, not trying. The pig's friend the wealthy C. Jimson Camphor and his butler, Bannister, have, as their hobby, the testing of maxims and proverbial wisdom: ". . . Most people," Mr. Camphor explains to Freddy (in *Freddy and Mr. Camphor*), "accept these proverbs as true. But Bannister and I don't agree with 'em. Ha! I guess we don't. We argue about them and when we can, we try them out . . ." (p. 33). Later, after Freddy has unjustly been accused of thievery and of trashing a houseboat, Bannister observes, "'You can't clean a pigsty without getting your hands dirty.' 'Eh? Is that a proverb, Bannister?' Mr. Camphor asked. 'Well, no, Sir, not exactly. That is, I just made it up.' 'Well, don't make up any more,' [Mr. Camphor orders]. 'We have plenty of old ones to examine into without making up new ones. And it's not a very good one, anyway.' 'Yes, sir,' said Bannister. But Freddy noticed that he wrote it down anyway . . ." (p. 114).

Equally as trying to Amos as Ben's maxims (one wonders if Mr. Camphor and Bannister ever tested *them*)—though hilarious to the reader—is "an enthusiasm which beset [Ben] . . . this was the study of what he called 'Electricity.'" The study begins innocently enough with the arrival of some glass tubes and a book of instructions sent by a London friend. These tubes, when rubbed by Ben with a piece of silk or fur, would produce "many strange and, to me, unpleasant effects." For the opinionated Amos this is understatement, especially as he goes on to explain that "Ben derived great amusement from rubbing a tube and touching it to the tip of my tail. Thereupon a terrible shock would run through my body. . . . This was bad enough, but my final rebellion did not come until he, in his enthusiasm, used the fur cap to rub the tube. And I was in the cap" (p. 40).

If this is bad, it will get worse. Ben, with typical hubris, decides "to give an exhibition of his achievements in the field." Unfortunately (for him), he leaves Amos alone in the hall he has rented for this purpose (since he has gone to have his hair curled, the reader may presume that vanity has triumphed over common sense), and Amos, "determined that no errors should mar this performance, since it meant so much to Ben . . ." (p. 44) "rectifies" a number of errors he finds in the wiring. The results are predictable: Both the Governor and the Fire Chief are nearly electrocuted.

Nothing daunted, Ben continues his experiments, bringing them closer to home, for, as he self-importantly points out to Amos, "the trouble with most people is that they lack the calm observation of the trained scientific mind." Since Lawson has by now established a pattern in which pomposity of any sort is punished by humiliation, the reader shivers—not from electrical shock, but from the pleasurable anticipation of the comeuppance to come. We are not disappointed. The ensuing display of terrifyingly untamed lightning reduces Ben—to Amos's and the reader's delight—to a quivering lump under the covers of his bed.

There is even more to come, though the conclusion of Ben's experiments is almost the conclusion of his relationship with Amos. So consumed with curiosity about the relationship of lightning and electricity is Ben that he betrays the mouse, stranding him at the top of a kite in an electrical storm. Finally restored to terra firma, Amos, in his turn, storms off without a word to Ben.

After several days' separation, Franklin, "most agreeable and apologetic" shows up at Amos's parents' house, where the mouse has sought refuge. He forswears further scientific experiments, explaining that he has been chosen to go to England to lay the case of the Colonists at the feet of the King and Parliament. He begs Amos to forgive him and accompany him. "Without you, Amos, I should be lost. Your advice and your wonderful facility for gathering information are more than ever necessary to me. What say you, Amos? I sail at dawn."

Readers grin with pleasurable anticipation of Amos's answer, for we know by now that with Amos, flattery will get you everywhere.

And sure enough: "It was a solemn moment," the mouse remembers, "but without an instant's hesitation I sprang to my feet. 'Liberty forever!' I shouted. 'I'm with you, Ben'" (pp. 63–64).

The reader may also reflect that if the mouse knows his man, the man, equally well, knows his mouse.

Ben's experiments with electricity occupy only three of the fifteen chapters of *Ben and Me*, but together they serve as a brilliant catalogue of the types, forms, and constructions of humor that inform the best of children's literature.

First of all there is the humor of character, and the exaggeration of personality characteristics that enhance that humor (the pomposities and vanities of Ben and Amos, the childlike enthusiasms of Ben's researches); then there is the delightful humor of anticipation, when an aspect of character sets in motion a situation that the reader recognizes will result in comic climax; there are the puncturing of pretentiousness, and the superiority the reader accordingly feels to those who have come a cropper; then there is the humor of scene, situation, and slapstick, for instance, Ben's "demonstration" that nearly electrocutes the Governor and the

Fire Chief—a situation whose humor is amplified by its poking fun at authority (think how much funnier this scene is with the grand, bewigged politician of a governor as its butt than it would have been if an ordinary citizen had been in the "hot seat." This point is underscored by the reluctance of the apprentice to stop grinding the machine that is shocking the Governor: "The lad, not an admirer of the Governor, ceased his efforts with some reluctance" (p. 46). Some readers may be made uneasy by the element of cruelty implicit in much of the humor described above. Certainly it is difficult to imagine the kindhearted Doctor Dolittle finding amusement in shocking any of his household animals with an electrified rod or, no matter how inflamed his scientific imagination was with curiosity, putting an animal's life in jeopardy in an electrical storm. Yet there are moments of cruelty in the Dolittle books: Consider the fidgit's story in *Voyages*: The fish recalls what happened to an elderly man "in whiskers and spectacles" (the stock comic image of the intellectual) whose only "sin" has been to see that the fidgit and his sister have "the proper food to eat, the right amount of light, and that the water in their tank [is] not too hot or too cold" (p. 208): ". . . he fell right into the water. . . . From this he was rescued by a sailor with a boat-hook; and the last we saw of him, the man in blue [a policeman] was dragging him away by the coat-collar, lecturing him . . ." (p. 215).

The Freddy books also, on occasion, employ a similar cruel humor, subjecting Freddy to numerous humiliations; in the very first of his adventures, *To and Again*, the pig—to be polite—reluctantly accepts a goat's invitation to eat thistles, and, of course, "As soon as he had taken the bite, he wished he hadn't . . . he coughed and sneezed and squealed and grunted and ran around and round in circles *while the other animals laughed*" (emphasis added; p. 115). Similarly, in *Freddy and the*

Ignormus he winds up in a prickly barberry bush not once but twice and has to put camphor ice on his scratches to make them stop smarting (p. 41), while in *Freddy and the Space Ship* (1953) he is thrown out of the phaeton and hits his nose on a rock (p. 40), and then, to compound the cruelty, only two pages later he is hit in the rear by a board and falls headfirst into a rain barrel "about half full of rain water" (pp. 42–43).

So there is cruelty, yes, but it is generally redeemed by the warmth of friendship and the generosity of spirit that prevail in all these books. When it isn't, the quality of the book suffers. Case in point: Lawson's second animal "biography," *I Discover Columbus*. The narrator this time is not a mouse but a parrot, Aurelio, whom Lawson, in another foreword, claims to have met while recovering from a spell of tropical fever at the Central American home of one Don Tomás. When the bird, now some five hundred years old, realizes the natives are celebrating Columbus Day and snorts, with some asperity, "Columbus, 'The Great Explorer,' Columbus, 'The Great Navigator,' 'The Great Admiral'—Bah!" the reader knows what is to come, and Lawson does not disappoint: "'"Colón," he was called in my day,' [the bird rants] 'plain Cristobal Colón—and I could tell you what a "Great Admiral" he was. I could tell you who *really* discovered the Americas, I could tell—'

"'Why don't you?' [Lawson] asked."

"'I think I will,' he rasped" (p. viii).

And so, of course, he does. And anyone who is tempted to doubt the accuracy of his recollection is reminded by Lawson that "There is a cold yellow gleam in those eyes, there is a keen curve to that huge beak, painfully like a pair of well-sharpened pruning shears, that somehow discourages any doubting of his word" (p. ix).

The trouble is that this cold, metallic sharpness informs not only Aurelio's character but his narrative as well, despite a nicely whimsical start: Aurelio is caught up in the "terrible Hurricane of 1491" and literally blown from Central America to Spain. There, at the Convent of La Rabida, he meets Columbus (or Colón, as he was then called). (Aurelio notes, by the way, that there still exists, in the upper reaches of the Magdalena [in Columbia], an ancient alligator who could tell you breathtaking tales of the destruction the hurricane wrought. It is irresistibly tempting to speculate that this "ancient alligator" might be The Grandfather of All the Alligators, who is the bête noir of the animals in *To and Again*. After all, he is also hugely old. "My dear," he advises Freddy's friend Henrietta the hen, "I am more than 800 years old. I was centuries old when Ponce de Leon came to Florida. . . . I remember Balboa well. . . . He made the same mistake you did—he mistook me for a log. But he was more fortunate than you. He got away with merely the loss of one of his boots . . . a delicious boot that was, too—old Spanish leather. I chewed on it for half a day" [p. 108].)

Unfortunately, once Aurelio meets Colón, the narrative quickly begins to bog down in the parrot's personal swamp of bad humor, bloated hubris, and downright nastiness. Given the conventions of animal satire, one may at first accept Aurelio's satirical contempt for human beings (of the monks he acidly notes, "As they shrieked and leaped about in astonishment it began to dawn on me that these poor benighted creatures had never seen a bird that could talk!" [p. 12]), but the reader quickly realizes that his contempt will never be tempered by warm feelings toward anybody or anything, save himself. Amos can be splenetic, but he demonstrates genuine fondness for Ben, for the white mouse Sophie, and for members of his family. Polynesia, Doctor Dolittle's parrot, who is also notably acid-tongued and occasionally bad-tempered, is, nevertheless, absolutely devoted to the Doctor and to ensuring his well-being. Aurelio is devoted only to himself ("Haven't you noticed what a sensation I, Aurelio, the Bird-That-Talks, have made in this stupid country of yours?" [p. 21]). The only thing he is generous with is his contempt, sharing it not only with Colón and the monks but with literally everyone he encounters. (He calls an innkeeper "You poor ignorant clod" [p. 26]. He refers to Ferdinand and Isabella as "these petty rulers" [p. 32].) Even other birds arouse his disdain: "They are a stupid breed, the pelicans" (p. 94). The Columbus Aurelio depicts is impossibly stupid and unsympathetically one-dimensional, motivated not by a personal vision but only by dreams of wealth and glory ("I was thinking of my titles and honors—and a crimson cloak" [p. 21]). He has to be tricked into going on his voyage of discovery and, once under way, becomes "the seasickest person who ever lived" (p. 83). Having finally attained the shores of the New World (thanks to the efforts of others), Columbus becomes a monster of self-importance: "As Governor General of these lands I hold power of life and death over every living being here. This includes Indians—and parrots. One more bit of insolence and I will have you put in chains!" (p. 102).

Not that any other character is much more sympathetic. King Ferdinand is a stupid blusterer who is viewed with contempt by his Queen: "Don't ask silly questions," she warns him, adding, "and *don't* trip over that rope" (p. 80). He has, moreover, the soul of a brigand: "'Do you mean to suggest,' [he storms to Aurelio] 'that I, Ferdinand, King of Spain, should make promises that will not be kept?' 'Exactly that,' I answered. 'Bird,' he said, 'you have more sense than all my Councilors put together'" (p. 46). This may be a joke (and a predictable one, at that), but there is nothing humorous about the dubious morality it suggests, for the promises that Aurelio has blithely suggested that Ferdinand make only to break are promises to be made to Columbus. Aurelio is, thus, betraying the man he has supposedly befriended. No surprise, though, since Aurelio is also depicted as being a common thief, stealing jewels from nobles to finance Columbus's expedition so that Isabella will not have to pawn *her* jewels.

As this suggests, Isabella is the only character Aurelio likes—perhaps because she is as heartlessly egocentric as he is. The bird is particularly taken with her habit of "passing her finger across her neck in a quaint little gesture that she often used . . ." (p. 40).

Two other characters arouse Aurelio's arguable sympathy: young Doña Maria Mercedes d'Acosta, a lady in waiting, and her suitor, Don Manuel Nicosa, a Captain of the Guard. Unfortunately when Aurelio tries to be avuncular with these two, he winds up being patronizing: María becomes that "cute little lady in waiting, Doña What's-her-name," and when the two long to return to Spain, it's, "All right, children, all right. . . . Old Aurelio the Great Arranger will just have to get to work again" (p. 107). Old Aurelio is the bird who came to dinner: Sheridan Whiteside without the wheelchair—or the wit!

The sour, mean-spirited tone of the book reaches its arguable nadir in the search for an admiral to assist Columbus in his voyage. Those who refuse are turned over to Torquemada "and his little friends." "'You are, perhaps,' [Ferdinand says] smoothly . . . 'familiar with the Inquisitors and their ways? You would, no doubt, prefer to have your fingernails drawn slowly, one by one, with red-hot pincers, or to swallow little pellets of molten lead?'

"'At least, Your Majesty,' the Admiral cried, in desperation, 'I shall die holy.'

"'Holy or in parts,' said Ferdinand, laughing grimly at his horrid joke" (p. 64–65). Horrid indeed. And too typical of the tone and ill-advised attempts at humor that dominate this least of Lawson's four animal biographies.

In retrospect it is no surprise that the publication of *I Discover Columbus* was greeted with "a lack of buyer enthusiasm."[14] But it is unfortunate that that should have postponed, for a decade, the writing and publication of the third biography, *Mr. Revere and I*, for Lawson had chosen Revere as his subject as early as July 1941, when he wrote to his editor about his excitement over his next "cock-eyed biography."[15] I say unfortunate since, as a work of fiction, this is probably the most fully realized book of the four, and as narrator, Revere's horse Sherry may be the most interesting in terms of her growth and development as a character. For her book is as much the story of how she is transformed from Scheherezade, once the most admired mount of the Queen's Own Household Cavalry, to plain Sherry, patriot and free horse, as it is the biography of Paul Revere (whom she doesn't even meet until page 42 of this 152-page book). When the reader first meets *her*, however, he encounters a soul mate to Amos, albeit a more refined one. If anything, Sherry ("onetime toast of the Mustardshire Fencibles") is even *more* self-satisfied than the mouse.

"Filled with military ardor and pride in the glory of His Majesty's armed might," (p. 5) Sherry has been shipped to the Colonies, along with her "Leftenant" master, Sir Cedric Noel Vivian Barnstable, Bart., to occupy the port of Boston. The reader has already realized two things: One is that this will be a *bildungsroman*. The second is that much of its humor will be based on the delicious dichotomy between what Sherry sees and what the reader perceives. Here, for example, is her description of her master (or as she puts it, "the perfect picture of the ideal military man"): ". . . tall and slender (not spindly, as some said), he had the true proud nose of the conqueror, rather like that of a puffin *but less elaborately colored*. He was blessed with splendid strong teeth not greatly different from my own. These were quite prominently displayed, because his mouth was usually open and his chin was merely a slight ripple in the flesh" (emphasis added; p. 6). He also has a "slight" speech impediment, "not quite a stammer or a stutter but more a combination of the two." This is how he talks:

"Wa-wa-wa-well, Sh-Sh-Sh-Sherry old girl . . . thththumbs up, old dear. . . ." As to how he looks, the disparity between Sherry's description of him and the reader's mental image of his appearance is enlarged by Lawson's helpful rendering of him (p. 5), which reveals him to look for all the world like Ichabod Crane with a severe malocclusion!

The Leftenant is aide-de-camp to Sir Dagmore Dalrymple, a sputtering, red-faced, usually apoplectic, beef-eating Colonel Blimp type. Both men may be heroes to Sherry, but to the reader, they are stock British comic types, caricatures in their exaggerated characteristics. (When the Leftenant is injured in a fall, the attending physician "greatly" fears a brain injury, telling the Colonel, "His responses are very vague and disconnected." In response the Colonel roars, "Egad, he's *always* that way. Seemed brighter than usual to me" [p. 32]. Though Lawson, as an artist, was praised for his fine and meticulous line, as a satirical writer he obviously used a very broad brush, indeed.)

Sherry's loyalty to her master and to the crown he serves acts as a set of figurative blinders, compromising her ability to see clearly either the true nature of the British forces or of the New World around her. "I seethed with rage at hearing, instead of the thunderous applause and cheers which usually greeted us, only an occasional jeer of . . . 'Yah, yah! Bloody-backs—bloody backs! 'Oo wants lobsters?'" (p. 16).

To make it even worse, from Sherry's obscured point of view "these churlish peasants" overcharge the Army for hay and grain. "So exorbitant were [the prices] that [the Royal Paymaster] was scarcely able to put aside more than 50 per cent of the disbursements for himself" (p. 19). Sherry obviously has many lessons ahead of her, some of them to be bitterly learned, before her "blinders" will be removed.

But first there is a season of false peace to make the contrast with what will come after even more dramatic: Sherry recovers from the horrors of her voyage to the New World. Winter passes. The weather grows more summery. The "high-spirited young Officers" go on picnics and amuse themselves with the pleasant diversion of "shooting at the rustics' poultry. They were also shot at occasionally by the rustics but took it all in the spirit of fun" (p. 24). Only one thing casts a shadow of foreboding: Leftenant Barnstable's "notoriously bad" play at cards and dice. And, sure enough, the inevitable night comes when he loses Sherry in a card game—not to Paul Revere, for, in plot terms, that would be premature. Sherry is still too much the blindly loyal Royalist, too proud of herself and of the British to be redeemed by even a Paul Revere.

No, Sherry's new owner is not Paul Revere but, instead, "Stinky" Nat Sime, "the proprietor of a noisome glue factory not far from the Common." Her initial reaction to this abrupt change of fortune is instructive: Musing that she could have tossed her new owner off her back "as easily as a sack of grain," Sherry concludes, "But naturally for a horse of my breeding this would never do. For one must never, never allow one's personal feelings to interfere in the perfect performance of one's horsely duties. [Col. Dalrymple's horse Ajax] expressed this so splendidly when he used to say, 'After all, my dear, like 'im or not your master is your master'" (p. 34). The reader greets this bit of "wisdom" with a good horse laugh, knowing already that Ajax is a self-important, pompous blowhard (not unlike *his* master, the Colonel!).

Thus begins a period of almost unbearable humiliation for Sherry, whose new job is to pull cartloads of fish heads, hoofs, horns, and other offal from the docks to the slaughterhouse and back. Subject to jeers and insults, ill-fed, ill-watered, and ill-housed, suffering from collar sores, Sherry's worst fear is that she will encounter her old Regiment. When this inevitably happens, she runs away, determined to hurl herself into the waters of the harbor. She doesn't get that far: Turning into a narrow street, she runs headlong into a wain and, along with her cart and her driver, winds up in a tangled mass on the sidewalk.

Inevitably Leftenant Barnstable arrives on the scene astride Ajax, that great, noble steed.

"Oh, Ajax," Sherry cries despairingly. "Surely *you* know me!"

His reply is coldly devastating: "I never speak to civilians."

The Leftenant is even more unfeeling: "Whu-whu-why don't you shoo-shoo-shoot the brute [i.e., Sherry]?" he demands.

"Shoot the brute? What's going on here?" roars not Paul Revere (not yet, not yet) but, instead, that firebrand Patriot Sam Adams.

And in a moment, the British are chased from the scene in a rain of very decayed codfish heads.

"In my bitter humiliation and disillusionment I could not bring myself to feel any great regret for this disgraceful insult to the King's uniform" (pp. 42–43).

Sherry's redemption has begun.

But she will not become a Patriot overnight. Such a transformation would be unbelievable. But when Adams gives her to Paul

Revere to settle a debt, the transformation in her physical circumstances is dramatic. She is fed "regularly and bountifully"; she always has an ample supply of fresh water; her stall is "immaculate," and she is curried, brushed, and rubbed incessantly. Gradually her disposition improves and her spirits are restored; "this was due," she admits, "to the loving attentions of the Revere family."

She also admits that she finds the Revere children "a great pleasure." "Altogether, it was a loving, kindly family . . . even though they were only middle-class tradespeople" (p. 48)! Compare this attitude with that of Amos, who proudly reports, "My own brothers and sisters had also progressed in the world . . . several of them lived in our immediate neighborhood, successful, solid tradespeople" (pp. 107–8).

Sherry is still a snob, but gradually even this begins to change, in part because she is a keen observer (an essential quality in biographers, be they bipeds or quadrupeds) and since her stall door opens into the Revere kitchen, which serves triple duty as kitchen, living room, and dining room and, moreover, opens into Revere's workshop immediately beyond, she is able to observe not only the Revere family but the comings and goings of others on commercial *and* political business. She notes that the Patriots always paid for the goods they ordered from the Reveres, "which, I am ashamed to say, our [British] officers did not" (p. 50). Revere, too, earns her admiration as "the busiest man I have ever seen. From dawn to dusk he worked in his shop . . . with his large family no opportunity to earn an honest shilling could be neglected" (p. 50).

Lawson himself was a prodigiously hard worker, laboring from nine A.M. to five or six P.M. seven days a week and holidays. He applied the same work ethic to his own patriotic efforts: "He worked terribly hard during the War years," Sue Inman notes.

"He made many trips, giving talks to sell war bonds."[16] Perhaps as a result, he suffered a heart attack; he alludes to this, rather obliquely, in his 1945 Newbery Medal acceptance speech for *Rabbit Hill* (The Viking Press, 1944): "I had been laid up for a while and hadn't been down to the studio for almost two months. . . ."[17]

Sherry soon observes that Mr. Revere is busy not only with work but with politics. His home is a regular gathering place for The Sons of Liberty, and such stalwarts as John Hancock, James Otis, and "of course" Sam Adams were sure to drop by "to talk politics and sedition." Though obviously a Patriot himself, Lawson could not resist the temptation to lampoon the Colonists as well as the British, and in the fiery Sam Adams he found a perfect target. Perpetually in debt (his motivation for presenting Sherry to Revere is as much the settling of his bill with the silversmith as it is his own patriotic urges), Adams finds every occasion an opportunity for giving a speech (he could be the long-lost brother of Charles the rooster in the Freddy books in this particular); when he isn't speaking, he's eating—usually Paul Revere's breakfast, which has been left on the table after Adams has appeared to call Revere off to his patriotic duties. Lawson's treatment of Adams serves two purposes, of course: One is to afford comic relief; the second is to provide an element of balance in his treatment of the British and, by contrast, to make Revere appear even more of a serious-minded, but generous and kindhearted, Patriot.

Adams is a convincing talker, however, as are the other Patriots, and Sherry, overhearing their conversations, finds herself thinking that "some of their arguments made many of their grievances seem quite justified. I was frightfully confused and upset" (p. 51).

She is even more upset by a visitor to the Revere kitchen, a British Sergeant named Giles Treadwell. It turns out that Revere is in the habit of helping British deserters to resettle in the Colonies. Treadwell has good reason to be "determined-er nor ever" to desert: In one of the book's most dramatic moments, he tears off his coat and shirt and turns "so that the light of the fire fell full on his back. From shoulders to waist he was striped with angry red and purple welts" (p. 52). Treadwell explains to the horrified Revere that he has received twenty-five lashes for failing to salute "a mincing Officer to suit his fancy taste." The officer? Sherry's former master, Leftenant Cedric Barnstable! The reader may find it hard to accept the buffoonish Barnstable as a convincing villain, but there is no discounting the drama both in the words and in the two-page picture Lawson has created (pp. 52–53). It is the first illustration in the book to offer a serious, realistic image from history and, accordingly, is even more powerful than its intrinsic subject. The sight of the welts and whip scars on the Sergeant's back make readers catch their breath, and Sherry, as she is pictured at the left of the picture, is equally disturbed; indeed, as she records, "I was fairly sickened at the sight."

Treadwell's is only the first such "traitorous performance" Sherry will observe ("it seemed to occur every few evenings"), but hearing the tales of inhuman treatment at the hands of British officers, Sherry finds she can now "thoroughly sympathize." "I *should* have been horrified and outraged [at these examples of disloyalty], but I could not be. I just became more confused and upset in my mind . . ." (p. 55).

She becomes even more confused when she realizes that "these misguided Colonials were actually preparing for armed resistance to the King" (p. 59). She describes the disorder of the Militia companies in formation and recalls Ajax's contempt for them.

And yet . . . "I did not like to think of Ajax now" (p. 62).

She observes, at second hand, the Boston Tea Party, the seriousness of which is relieved by the contrapuntal humor of Paul Revere's elderly mother's thirst for a good cup of "real English tea." The joke is capped when the elderly lady appears triumphantly in the doorway with a teacup half filled with "real English tea, the finest Bohea."

Where did she get it? "Out of your silly Indian costume," she gleefully tells her chagrined son, "out of the creases and the torn lining." Talk about Yankee ingenuity. . . . The joke has a second punchline: "There's more, too," Mrs. Revere cackles, "but I'm saving that for Mr. Sam Adams. *It* came out of your shoes" (p. 79).

The Tea Party will result in more than Mrs. Revere's having a good cup of tea. It will finally usher in a sea change in Sherry's attitudes, converting her from a Royalist to a Patriot. It begins with the news that the King, in retaliation for the Tea Party, plans to close Boston harbor. Reflecting on what this would mean to the "dear Revere children" and what privations they would have to endure during the "bitter Boston winters," Sherry, for the first time in her life, "began to have doubts as to the divine wisdom of the King and his advisers. The glory of his Armed Forces, its Officers and Gentlemen, began to seem shoddy and tarnished" (p. 91). The news of an impending action is in itself not sufficiently dramatic to serve as a catalyst for Sherry's final change, though. That comes eleven pages later, when she and Mr. Revere, astride her, encounter none other than Leftenant Barnstable riding Ajax. The latter "glares" at Sherry. "Deserter!" he snorts. "Traitor! Spy!" (p. 102). Revere attempts to pass on, but Barnstable calls to his Sergeant to "Sta-sta-sta-stop him."

And, at last, the moment the reader has been waiting for with mounting excitement happens:

"Until that moment I had not fully realized how glorious it was to be free . . . free of callous Officers, stupid, overfed stable-mates—like Ajax!

"In a great blinding flash I knew that I would die rather than exchange my new-found liberty for that old prison-like existence I had once thought so glorious. I was a free horse! I was a Colonial! I was a Patriot, my life dedicated to the ideals of Liberty and Freedom!" (p. 103).

She rears, slashing wickedly at the Sergeant and, with a "vicious kick" on Ajax's hock, speeds away . . . to freedom.

There is significant historic incident yet to come, including Mr. Revere and Sherry's midnight ride (and one final encounter with Barnstable and Ajax), but it all seems oddly anticlimactic now that Sherry's figurative blinders have finally fallen off. Now that Sherry is committed to liberty, much of the conflict of character that has provided drama and humor to the book has been vitiated. The book ends—as does *Ben and Me*—with Sherry (like her predecessor Amos) full of years and honors enjoying the much-deserved rest that her quiet life now offers. Order has returned to both the Franklin and Revere households, and raucous laughter has been replaced with quiet smiles. (At least one of these smiles belongs to the reader, when Amos patiently explains to Ben that he must retire as his adviser: "You see the responsibilities I have now, all these eager young minds needing my guidance and instruction." The humor here lies in the reader's imagining "all these eager young minds" grinding their figurative teeth in frustration at this old bore's offering them endless advice and gratuitous instruction.)

There would be a fourth animal biography, but after the richness of *Mr. Revere and I* it, too, seems anticlimactic. *Captain Kidd's Cat* was published in 1956, the year before Lawson died. It would be the second-to-last book he completed (the last, *The Great Wheel*, is his tribute to the opportunities America offered to her nineteenth-century immigrants). In its tone it is more like *I Discover Columbus* than *Ben and Me* or *Mr. Revere and I*.

The narrator this time is a cat named McDermot who is distinguished by his sour disposition and the ruby ring he wears in his left ear. In the obligatory foreword, he rants, "'Captain Kidd the Pirate,' 'Kidd the Buccaneer,' 'Kidd the Murderer.' *Rats!*" The reader infers, correctly, that once again there will be a whole lot of debunkin' goin' on. Unlike Aurelio, however, McDermot is not intent on destroying a reputation but restoring it. The underlying incongruity of this "biography" will be that Kidd was not a pirate at all but a respectable and prosperous New York merchant. ("Bill Kidd was no more pirate than my Aunt Tabitha, that lives in Wapping," McDermot sniffs.) "The one wrong thing Bill Kidd did was to trust his friends, high and low, and try to do right by 'em," McDermot explains (p. 4). Perhaps it is this tone of righteous indignation that compromises the book's comic capacities. Or perhaps it is Lawson's own anger at the moral corruption of politics. The most telling paragraph in the book is Kidd's eruption to McDermot: "And now politics is mixed up in this miserable affair . . . politics and intrigue, jealousies and greed. Whig fighting Tory, Tory knifing Whig. The East India Company fighting anyone and everything that threatens their outrageous profits—and here we are in the middle of it, Mac, like wheat between their bloody grindstones. Should I be in their way, they'll crush me, Mac, crush me with no more thought than they'd crush a bothersome insect" (p. 59).

Lawson's later work is not alone in its darkness. Lofting's last book, *Doctor Dolittle and the Secret Lake* (J. B. Lippincott, 1948), is infected with what Edward Blishen calls his "growing despair about the future of life on earth."[18] And two of Walter R. Brooks's last three Freddy books (*Freddy and the Flying Saucer Plans*, 1956, and *Freddy and Simon the Dictator*, 1957) are, at times, almost vicious in their anger at the idiocies of politics and the human thirst for power (as reflected in the animal dictatorship's mirror of caricature).

McDermot, as narrator, is not the least humorous of the four "biographers," but he is, perhaps, the most passive. He does almost nothing to advance the narrative, and his participation in the unfolding proceedings is largely limited to his clawing Kidd's leg to alert him to possible perfidy in a companion—and even then Kidd is usually already aware of it. Indeed, in two of the three final chapters McDermot is reduced to the role of passive auditor as, in page after page of exposition, Kidd simply tells him what has happened at his various trials for piracy. If Lawson had only contrived a way to get McDermot into the courtroom so the cat could have dramatically re-created the proceedings, the book would have been stronger. Lawson does try to create humor in the essential incongruity of Kidd's character at home, where he is henpecked by and terrified of his termagant wife, and his character at sea: "It was good, too," McDermot reflects, "to see how fast Bill shed his Pearl Street meekness and became a man again" (p. 40). Good, perhaps, but for the reader unbelievable. Lawson's problem is not that he must make Kidd a sympathetic sailor but that he tries to make him heroic, too. "A Real Captain Is Kidd" is the title of one of the chapters. But the reader cannot forget his earlier depiction as a hapless Milquetoast and cat's-paw to his friends, including King William, who have no difficulty in persuading him to undertake for the Crown a mission that contains the seeds of Kidd's ultimate destruction: Determined to rid the seas of pirates, the King has commissioned a new ship, the *Adventure Galley*, to go on a pirate-hunting expedition. This is bad news not only for the pirates ("The Red Sea Brethren," p. 15) but for the merchants who buy booty from them. The solution to this commercial conundrum is a study in hypocrisy and questionable morality: The King will appoint as captain of the *Adventure Galley* a man who is sympathetic to the pirates and will studiously avoid capturing so much as one man jack of 'em. However, since the King and his cronies have purchased shares in the expedition and expect a hearty return on their investment, the captain will be expected to capture honest ships that have the misfortune to be sailing under the French flag, since France is presently at war with England— in other words, the *Adventure Galley* will become a privateer herself! This is very convoluted indeed, and Kidd—who has, of course, been persuaded to assume the captaincy of the *Adventure Galley*—has reservations, especially when the King's friend suggests that he just might consider occasionally capturing a rich Moorish ship that is *not* flying under the French flag. "That would be piracy," Bill snaps, "and I'm no pirate." "Quite so, quite so," Livingston agrees. However, ". . . *should* such an unfortunate error occur—think nothing of it. The King and his friends . . . can cover up any such irregularity . . ." (p. 28). Since we already know from McDermot's foreword that the cat will ultimately sell the ruby ring out of his ear to buy Kidd a decent shirt for his hanging, we also know that the seeds of Kidd's destruction have been sown and that he will ultimately be betrayed by his "friends." There is very little humor in that, although there is ample opportunity for sour satire. "Poor Bill," New York's Governor Fletcher laughs. "You're only used to dealing with pirates and privateers. This is your first brush with the perfumed footpads of the court" (p. 34).

We have already met "perfumed footpads" in *Ben and Me*, in which Amos's view of the French court is consistent with

Governor Fletcher's. The difference, however, is that *Ben and Me* offers a burlesque view of the court's pomposities and the worst that happens is that Ben will be snubbed by the French fops. In *Captain Kidd's Cat*, however, the specter of Kidd's eventual hanging looms like a black cloud over the entire narrative. The gloomy attitude that prevails is seldom lifted by humorous incident. On the contrary, a cholera epidemic decimates the crew; a sympathetic old cooper is murdered by natives ("There was a long sickening scream . . . that ended in a horrid gurgling noise" [p. 73]); there is mutiny; and ultimately there is betrayal: "They decided to make you the scapegoat," Kidd's friend Campbell tells him. "You are marked for the sacrifice" (pp. 121–22). Honest Kidd refuses to believe that Lord Bellomont (sic), the newly appointed Governor of New York, and—by extension—the King himself could thus betray a trust. Of course they could, and so Kidd's next stop is Newgate Prison. "Well, Mac, old cat," Kidd says, "Campbell was right. Put not your trust in princes" (p. 126). (The heavy-handedly ironic title of this chapter is "The Word of a Nobleman.") At book's end, Kidd is dead and McDermot, like Amos and Sherry, is living in comfortable retirement. The reader is glad for him but can summon up no emotion stronger, since McDermot as a character is the least interesting of the four animal biographers.

Given the gloominess of the book's overall tone and the seriousness of the incidents that comprise the narrative, Lawson must resort for what little humor lightens its pages to humorous simile: Mrs. Kidd is "pleasant as a crocodile" (p. 28), and Kidd is "like a mouse, squeaking in a thunderstorm" (p. 35), or "busy as a tavern pot boy of a Saturday night" (p. 35). A sailor is "hoarse as a crow from his singing" (p. 51), and the drunken ship's doctor is "limp as a dead eel" (p. 42). Or to invective: "Where is that imbecile sot, [the ship's doctor]?" Kidd thunders (p. 68). The Bosun's answer is amusing in its illiteracy: "'E's strickly non compass mentus, sir, not to say very horse de combat . . ." or to sarcasm: "An awe-inspiring aggregation of pirates you make," Kidd sneers at his crew, "terrifying truly. The greengrocers and toffee vendors must quake in their boots when you step ashore. I thought I had a crew of seamen, not pickpockets" (p. 71).

Lawson's loathing for royalty (the ultimate authority) reaches its inarguable apogee in this book, but it has been a feature in all the books preceding it. We have also seen how Aurelio treats Ferdinand and Isabella and how Sherry comes to view the Royal Army. The French court fares no better in *Ben and Me*. The artificiality of court life is anathema to Amos (and to Lawson, by extension), who detests its foppery. Ben, of course, is quite taken with it, and Amos is horrified by Ben's preparations for the Fourth of July ball: "He fluttered about from one tailor to another as excitedly as a young belle preparing her trousseau. . . . He even had his nails manicured. This was really alarming" (p. 86).

Later (p. 95) Ben is "in a twitter of excitement over his new clothes." In the illustrations, clothes and their appurtenances provide wonderful raw material for comical exaggeration, most notably the headdress of Madame Brillon: "The powdered curls, rising to a height of four feet above her head, were arranged to represent the waves of the ocean. Surmounting these was a full rigged ship with an American flag at the masthead . . ." (p. 93). This is not only a humorous use of historical fact (women of the French court actually did wear such elaborate headdresses) but a clever narrative device, since it develops that the ship will house a contingent of Swedish mice who will help Amos rescue the white mouse Sophia's children; it also echoes Ben's old fur hat, which has served as Amos's aerie and home. (That fine contemporary author-illustrator Deborah Nourse Lattimore has done an homage to this device in her witty book *The Woman with the Ship on Her Head* [Harcourt, Brace, 1990].)

Lawson allows grudging admiration for the fighting skills of the French mice: "Pampered fops though they are, there are many skilled swordsmen among them" (p. 89) (of course, this also heightens the drama). However, he returns to ridicule when the King and Queen of France both faint at the invasion of their court by fighting mice—indeed, the King "was rather badly trampled by the fleeing ladies of the court."

The double-page spread that illustrates this indignity provides a visual inventory of Lawson's great gifts as an illustrator and the style in which he worked. There is, first of all, the loving detail of execution. Lawson himself wrote of "the infinite detail which it is possible to put into a drawing to enhance the scene,"[19] and it was his particular gift to be able to incorporate such telling detail without compromising the clarity of the picture. There is a (perhaps) apocryphal story of a small boy who, after viewing an exhibition of illustrations, said, "I like *his* [Lawson's] best, because he draws them up nice and neat, and you can tell what they mean."

You can, indeed. Lawson came to children's book illustration from fifteen years in the world of commercial art, a world that rewards accessibility and a strong narrative sense. To that Lawson added painstaking care ("I have never seen any reason why a drawing for a child's book should be any less carefully planned or worked out than one for the most important scientific article . . ."[20]). One can see the careful planning that preceded the loving execution of *this* picture and its extraordinary detail: In the foreground are the carefully drawn fighting ship's rats of John Paul Jones, carrying a tattered Old Glory. On the left is a black drape framing the scene. The framing effect is carried out as the eye travels around the perimeter of the scene depicting the comic chaos of the court in its elaborate confusion, including the Queen in a dead faint across two thrones. There are candelabra and more curtains, vaulted arches leading off into other rooms of the castle, and, of course, tiny squadrons of fighting mice almost geometrically disposed across the floor and the steps to the throne. The fleeing court comes closer on the right, and in the right foreground is a fleeing dandy holding on, for dear life, to his wig. And there in the left foreground, "dripping mice," is Ben himself, looking in his perplexity like a shamefaced schoolboy. His expression is priceless and remarkable in its execution, since it consists of nothing more than four dots (for eyes, nose, and mouth) and two tiny lines for eyebrows, which have risen almost to the top of his head. Lawson offers this comic understatement in hilarious counterpoint to the elaborately detailed surroundings and, indeed, even to the finery that clothes Ben's dumpy body.

Lawson echoes Lofting and Brooks in his respect for his audience: "Children are *really* smart," he wrote. "You can't fool *them*. . . . I have never, I hope, insulted the intelligence of any child."[21] This attitude he applied with equal force to his words *and* to his illustrations: "The moment any one's work looks as though it were obviously done for children then we are talking down to children, we are talking baby talk with illustrations which I think is low and stupid. I think that trying to *rise* to the levels demanded by the clear ideals of children is a far greater task and a much more satisfying accomplishment than meeting the muddle-headed demands of their elders."[22] That he always strove to rise to those levels may be one of the most significant reasons for the lasting value of his work.

Another is surely the enduring nature of many of the values it celebrated. For while Lawson certainly poked fun at the Founding Fathers, he revered the best values they espoused and traits they evinced. "Liberty and justice forever!" cry the Revolutionary mice as they fight their way across the floor of the French court.

Lawson lived most of his life not in a court but in the Connecticut countryside. (In *Mr. Revere and I* he couldn't resist a gentle poke at his neighbors: Sherry notes that "Even the inhabitants of Connecticut, noted for their surliness and sharp dealings, were kind and helpful—moderately" [p. 82].) And he was as much a Yankee Patriot as was Amos. He was, moreover, a marvelously keen observer of the New England landscape. In the Foreword to another of his books, *Watchwords of Liberty* (Little, Brown, 1943), he recalls that "Today . . . I went up on our hill at noon and looked out over a bit of New England."

He looked out over "a bit of New England" in most of his books and found there much that epitomized the best in the American national character, and that was as enduring as the rocks and rugged hills of the landscape itself.

Helen D. Fish called him "an illustrator in the great tradition."[23] It is the traditional and enduring qualities of strength and goodness, of hard work and love of small animals, of liberty and justice, that—along with an enlivening leaven of humor—inform the best of Lawson's work and insure that it, too, will endure.

Frog and Toad . . . and Friendship

"I'm a small adventurer."
—"An Interview with Arnold Lobel"

It is neither politics nor patriotism but friendship that provides subject and theme for those little masterpieces by Arnold Lobel, the Frog and Toad books (although friendship may resemble politics in one respect, in that both are exercises in the art of compromise). And it is not hard-edged satire that provides their humor but rather character, and the situations that character and personality at work create. Lobel's biographer, George Shannon, points out that Lobel "based his humor on recognition of behavior rather than on gags and jokes. It is impossible to share the laughter of a Frog and Toad story without telling the entire story."[24]

There were twenty stories all together, spread equally among four books—five stories per book. The first, *Frog and Toad Are Friends*, was published in 1970; the second, *Frog and Toad Together*, appeared in 1972; the third, *Days with Frog and Toad*, in 1976 and the fourth, *Frog and Toad All Year*, in 1979, adding a grace note to the end of the decade. All four were innovative entries in Harper & Row's I Can Read series, expanding the boundaries of the early-reader genre and earning critical praise and honors in the process. *Frog and Toad Are Friends* was a Caldecott Honor Book and a finalist for the National Book Award; perhaps more significantly, the second title, *Frog and Toad Together*, was a Newbery Honor Book—significant because the Newbery honors excellence in writing, not in illustrating. Such an accolade not only celebrates Lobel's artistry with words—as the Caldecott Honor had with pictures—but implies his respect for the intelligence of his audience—a respect he himself articulated to an interviewer: "I don't use a controlled vocabulary at all. I wouldn't dream of it."[25] Echoing the esteem of Lofting, Brooks, and Lawson for children, Lobel marveled, "They're amazing. Once they bite into reading, they'll read anything . . . even if they come to a word that they have to sort out and fight with a bit."[26]

Lobel takes this notion a step further when he says, "All of the Frog and Toad stories are based on adult preoccupations. . . . I think that's why adults also enjoy them . . . it's because they're really adult stories slightly disguised as children's stories."[27]

Robert Lawson had made a similar point thirty years earlier: Recalling that he had been creating children's books for twenty-five years, he noted, "In all that time I have never, as far as I can remember, given one moment's thought as to whether any drawing that I was doing was for adults or for children. I have never changed one conception or line or detail to suit the supposed age of the reader. And I have never, in what writing I have done, changed one word or phrase of text because I felt it might be over the heads of children."[28]

Walter R. Brooks anticipated this point, too, when he wrote, "The books [children] like are the books that grownups can enjoy with them, books that after they themselves are grown up, they can reread with pleasure. That is certainly so with the books I liked best as a child. That is why I hope that my stories will amuse the grownups. For if they don't, they certainly won't amuse the children."[29]

Both are talking about a point Lobel addresses more specifically: "It seems to me the one thing that doesn't change much as we grow older is our sense of humor. I think a child's sense of humor and an adult's sense of humor are rather the same [although] our points of reference become larger. But the basics: we laugh at incongruity and we laugh at lack of dignity. If a man's pants fall down, everybody laughs, children [and] adults."[30]

Lobel makes these points implicitly in an early Frog and Toad story, "A Swim" (*Friends*). The premise is simple: Frog and Toad go down to the river and, it being a beautiful day, decide to go for a swim. The incongruity arises when Toad announces that he will go behind some rocks to put on his bathing suit. A toad in a bathing suit? The idea is incongruously funny. But Lobel takes it another step, adding a dose of that lack of dignity. Toad warns Frog, "After I put on my bathing suit, you must not look at me until I get into the water" (p. 41). Why? Not, as the reader might at first suppose, because of childlike modesty (reinforced by Toad's changing behind the rocks). Instead it is "'Because I look funny in my bathing suit. That is why,' said Toad" (p. 42). Frog obediently covers his eyes and doesn't peek until Toad is in the water. Other creatures are not as faithful. First "A turtle came along the riverbank" (p. 44).

Toad is anxious that the turtle not see him in his bathing suit. However, instead of initiating action himself, he orders *Frog* to "tell that turtle to go away" (p. 44). And Frog complies. Had Toad been alone, would *he* have asked the turtle to go away? Probably not. For consider that when other animals, hearing that Toad looks funny in his bathing suit, line the riverbank waiting for a look and a laugh, Toad resorts to . . . stasis, announcing that he will stay "right here" (in the river) until they go away. Of course this only increases their curiosity, and they don't leave—despite Frog's pleas on his friend's behalf, "Please . . . please go away" (p. 48).

Ultimately Toad *will* leave the water. Not because of any act of volition on his part but rather as a reaction to the increasing coldness of the water. Predictably, the waiting animals then *do* laugh at Toad. And so does the reader, for Toad has been right all along. He *does* look incongruously funny (and definitely *un*dignified) in his old-fashioned, knee-length, striped bathing suit. What *is* surprising is that Frog joins the others in laughing at Toad. Traditional interpretations of friendship would forbid a friend's laughing at his friend's discomfiture. Consider the episode in Brooks's *Freddy Rides Again* in which the Bean Farm animals learn the guilty secret of the newcomer Arthur, the cat: His owner's nickname for him is the humiliating "Sweetie-Pie." Freddy says to his friend Jinx, another cat, who is the one who has spilled the . . . beans, "'I won't let him know you told us. We don't want him going around feeling embarrassed every time he sees one of us.'

"'I suppose you're right,' said the cat. 'But I hate to pass up a good joke.'

"'No joke is good if it hurts somebody's feelings,' said [the horse]" (p. 59).

Similarly, in Lois Lowry's *Anastasia Krupnik* (1979) we read, "Often Anastasia's parents had told her that there is laughing *with* someone, and there is laughing *at* someone, and one is okay but the other is not" (p. 46).

On the other hand, despite being laughed at by his best friend, Toad does not betray any embarrassment or hurt feelings. Instead his reaction is one of vindication: ". . . you *do* look funny in your bathing suit," says Frog.

"Of course I do," says Toad. He sounds smug and, as we can see in Lobel's drawing of him at the foot of the chapter, he also *looks* smug and even self-satisfied (p. 52). Of course, he may go to bed when he gets home, even though it's the middle of the day! "Toad," Lobel has noted, "is a neurotic . . . like most of us. He's the kind of person who, if something goes wrong, goes to bed. . . . That's a very rational way of dealing with one's problems. You go to bed and you wake up."[31]

Toad's relationship with his bed is not completely a function of his healthy neurosis, however, but a reflection of Lobel's faithfulness to Toad's realistic animal nature: Toads hibernate, a fact that informs the very first Frog and Toad story, "Spring" (*Friends*). Ebullient Frog arrives at Toad's house anxious to share the spring with his friend. "Wake up," he shouts. "It is spring."

Toad's response is a characteristically saturnine "Blah" (p. 4).

Dragged out of bed and onto the front porch by the forcefully friendly Frog, Toad is blinded by the sun. "I cannot see anything," he complains (p. 7).

Frog's answer is telling: "Don't be silly. . . . What you see is the clear warm light of April. And it means that we can begin a whole new year together, Toad" (p. 8).

For once, friendship is less important to Toad than his systemic need for sleep.

"Come back again and wake me up at about half past May," he grumps (p. 11).

"But Toad," Frog protests, "I will be lonely until then" (p. 12).

Toad does not answer, having already fallen asleep.

This is an interesting twist on their typical relationship as it will develop in later stories. For it is usually Toad who is anxious about the status of their friendship. Indeed, the ultimate Frog and Toad story, "Alone" (*Days*), is all about Toad's misapprehension of Frog's desire to be alone, thinking (wrongly) it means that Frog no longer wants to be his friend.

How Frog deals with Toad's de facto rejection in this first story is significant in what it reveals about his character. Instead of going to bed in the middle of the day as Toad would have done, he leaps into *action* and contrives a way to fool Toad into believing that it is May.

"'Why, it *is* May!' said Toad as he climbed out of bed. Then he and Frog ran outside to see how the world was looking in the spring" (p. 15).

Though there are many differences between the Frog and Toad books and Kenneth Grahame's *Wind in the Willows* (as enumerated by Shannon), there is one overriding similarity: In a sense Frog is the Water Rat to Toad's Mole. Frog, in his upbeat, active, outgoing, joyful way, is the more well adjusted of the two. But Toad, in his neurotic, saturnine, worrywart way, is the more interesting character and the one whose eccentricities provide much of the books' humor—be it situational or incongruous.

For consider that when Toad *is* stirred to action, the result usually involves physical humor and misadventure. In the second Frog and Toad story, "The Story," Frog—uncharacteristically in bed under the weather—asks Toad for a story. Toad, of course, can't think of one and so resorts to a variety of strategies, each more exaggerated than the last: First he walks up and down on the porch; then—when that proves fruitless—he stands on his head. Inspiration is still elusive, so he pours "many" glasses of water on his head. Finally he bangs his head against the wall.

By this time Frog feels better but Toad—understandably—feels "terrible." He replaces his friend in bed and, in his turn, asks for a story.

The witty and resourceful Frog has no need to resort to exaggerated, slapstick physicality for inspiration. He simply tells Toad the story of Toad's own fruitless efforts to tell *him* a story.

"How was that, Toad?" Frog asks at story's end (p. 27).

There is no answer, for Toad has—predictably—fallen asleep. Order returns to Toad's world when he is asleep. But when he is awake, Toad invites comic disorder into his activities by inevitably—as we have just seen—taking things too far. We've seen how he tries to conjure up a story for Frog. On another occasion Frog gives him seeds to start a garden. Not content to let nature operate at its appointed pace, Toad urges the seeds to grow by shouting encouragement, by reading them stories, singing songs, reading poems, and playing music—all to no avail. It is not until he falls asleep that the seeds begin to grow.

On still another occasion, when Frog is late for a Christmas

Eve rendezvous, Toad immediately begins imagining the worst: Frog has fallen into a hole, Frog is lost in the woods, Frog is being chased by a big animal. In fact, as it turns out, he has only been delayed because he has been busy wrapping Toad's present.

And yet there is often a perverse logic in Toad's excesses. In "A List" (*Together*), Toad makes a list of things to do today. Unfortunately a strong gust of wind blows the list away. Toad refuses to run after it. Why? "Because," wails Toad, "running after my list is not one of the things that I wrote on my list of things to do!" (p. 14).

In his illogical logic, his absurd overreactions, his fears and anxieties, Toad is often childlike. To his good fortune he has in Frog not only a thoughtful best friend but, more often than not, an ideal big brother who patiently tells stories of when he was small (like Toad, the reader may infer), plans adventures, and makes decisions. In one story ("Down the Hill," from *All Year*) he even dresses Toad: "Frog pushed a coat down over the top of Toad. Frog pulled snowpants up over the bottom of Toad. He put a hat and scarf on Toad's head" (pp. 6–7).

Toad's response is funny in its childish overdramatization: "Help!" he cries. "My best friend is trying to kill me!"

Energetic Frog then drags Toad outside to enjoy the winter . . . whether Toad wants to or not. Frog announces they will ride down "this big hill" on his sled. When Toad . . . uh, *demurs*, Frog—in true big brother fashion—says reassuringly, "Do not be afraid. . . . I will be with you on the sled" (p. 8).

In fact, though Toad doesn't at first realize it, Frog falls off the sled almost immediately. However, so long as Toad continues to think Frog is behind him, all is well (how many children have learned to ride a bicycle by thinking an older sibling is walking along behind, holding on to the rear of the bike?). The sled rushes past trees and rocks, it leaps over snowbanks, and Toad has a grand time. "Winter is fun!" he exults (p. 11). But then disaster strikes. Toad discovers "I AM ALL ALONE!" (p. 13). He immediately loses control of the sled, which hits a tree and then a rock and finally dives into the snow. In fine, slapstick fashion Toad hurtles off and winds up buried in a snowbank.

Frog runs to the rescue (of course) and tries to sell Toad on the idea that he did very well alone.

Toad is not buying this, however. "I did not" is his flat rejoinder. "But there is one thing that I can do all by myself."

"'What is that?' asked Frog. [The reader is already enjoying the humorous anticipation of knowing exactly what Toad's answer will be. And sure enough:]

"'I can go home,' said Toad. 'Winter may be beautiful, but bed is much better'" (p. 17).

Toad, in fact, seems to spend more time asleep than any other character in children's literature—with the possible exception of Sleeping Beauty and . . . Freddy the Pig, who does most of his sleeping sitting up in his overstuffed chair, "thinking," as he euphemistically puts it.

In fact, much of the action of one of the most interesting stories in the Frog and Toad cycle takes place when Toad is asleep in bed ("The Dream," in *Together*). He dreams that he is onstage wearing a costume, while Frog is in the audience, watching.

A strange voice from far away says, "PRESENTING THE GREATEST TOAD IN ALL THE WORLD!" (p. 53).

Toad takes a deep bow and launches a glorious one-man variety show. Such dreams of glory are not uncommon among characters in children's literature: Junior Blossom in Betsy Byars's *The Not-Just-Anybody Family* (1986) has a dream in which he performs a harmonica solo (shades of Robert McCloskey's *Lentil*) with "a huge orchestra. This was his one chance to be a star . . ." (p. 93). And Jane Moffat's new best friend, Nancy, admits, "I dream I'm a great singer. I'm on the platform and all the theater is clapping and clapping" (*The Moffats*, 1941, pp. 256–57). Frog greets Toad's performance with enthusiastic applause, yet each feat Toad performs diminishes Frog until the latter—normally the larger of the two (like a [literally] big brother) is "so small that he could not be seen or heard" (p. 59).

Though it is Frog who has become physically small, it is he himself, Toad realizes, who has been diminished. Shouting "Come back, Frog. . . . I will be lonely!" (p. 60), he wakes up to discover that Frog is standing by his bed.

In the waking world, we see, Toad need never be lonely. He looks at the sunshine streaming through the window and then, significantly, speaks to Frog, whose friendship also lights his life.

"Frog," he says, "I am so glad that you came over."

Frog's answer is simple yet vastly reassuring: "I always do."

The two eat a hearty breakfast and then spend "a fine, long day together" (pp. 63–64).

For Frog and Toad, then, friendship is the comfort and joy of being together. C. S. Lewis, in his book *The Four Loves*, says friends stand together "in an immense solitude."[32] It is the kind of "immense solitude" Frog and Toad experience when sitting "alone together" as Lobel describes it more than once. Certainly other animals do inhabit the softly green-and-brown garden world of Frog and Toad, but they are incidental to the stories, which are uniformly about incidents that inform the two animals' lives . . . *together*.

On the other hand, it is also true that the two do have separate homes and conduct the business of their individual lives separately (Frog works in his garden; Toad—well, Toad *sleeps*!), but in only one of the twenty stories do they fail to come together, and even in that story, "The Surprise" (*All Year*), the two are together in the sense that each is individually working to surprise the other by raking the leaves from the other's front yard. A wind will come along later and blow all the carefully raked leaves back across the lawns, but Frog and Toad are unaware of that. Thinking with pleasurable delight about how surprised the other will be, each goes to bed happy. (The reader empathetically shares their pleasure but also experiences the rueful humor of imagining the *real* surprise each will discover the next day.)

In fact, togetherness is such a major part of their relationship that when Toad one day finds a note on Frog's door saying that he (Frog) has gone out, wanting to be alone, Toad can only say, "Frog has me for a friend. Why does he want to be alone?" ("Alone," in *Days*, p. 52).

In fact, the idea of solitude is so unthinkable to Toad that he can only presume that Frog must be "very sad" (being together = happiness; being alone = sadness) and takes it upon himself to cheer his friend up. First he fixes a basket of sandwiches and a pitcher of iced tea; then he hurries to the riverbank (he has earlier seen Frog sitting alone on an island in the middle of the river). Asking a passing turtle to carry him to the island, Toad explains, "Frog is there. He wants to be alone."

As a surrogate for the reader, the turtle asks the question we would: "If Frog wants to be alone . . . why don't you leave him alone?"

Toad reacts with childlike egocentricity, presuming that Frog's solitude *must* be about him. "Maybe he does not want me to be his friend anymore," he worries (pp. 58–59).

And so Toad arrives at the island in an agony of apologies for all the "dumb things" he does. As if to demonstrate, he slips off the turtle's back and "with a splash" falls into the river.

Frog must (once again) rescue him. That essential bit of business taken care of, Frog then explains that he has wanted to be alone "to think about how fine everything is"—including his friendship with Toad, who sheepishly admits, "I guess that is a very good reason for wanting to be alone."

The two stay on the island all afternoon, ". . . two close friends sitting alone together" (pp. 62–64).

In a—dare one say "psychological"?—sense it is important that Frog and Toad be together, since they represent disparate parts of Lobel's own character and only together do they form a coherent whole. When asked by Geraldine DeLuca, "Do you see yourself more as Frog than as Toad?" his hasty reply was "Both, both."[33]

On another occasion he stated that "All the Frog and Toad stories are based on specific things in my life."[34] This is what lends the stories their wonderful emotional truth. Lobel obviously recognized that: "It is those books," he once wrote, "that have a subjective importance to their authors that turn out to be the good ones. When I can put myself into a frame of mind to be able to share with the reader my problems and my own sense of life's travail, then I discover that I am working in top form. It is a devious process. It involves some amount of duplicity, this transformation of adult preoccupation into stories to which children will respond."[35]

What made it work—although Lobel didn't make the connection himself—was something he wrote in the same essay about picture-book creators: "As a group we seem to cling to the need for the kind of imaginative playing that childhood allows."[36] The need for imaginative play, the spirit of such play, the state of being "in play," as Max Eastman put it—all underscore and contribute to the humor not only of Frog and Toad but of all the books we have discussed so far, by authors as various as Hugh Lofting and Walter R. Brooks, Robert Lawson and Arnold Lobel. The adult author becomes metamorphosed into an animal and, in the process, becomes a child. The result—in tone, in spirit, in incident, in character—is humor. It is delight. And what is more delightful than friendship?

Friendship was obviously important to Arnold Lobel. It is important to Frog and Toad. It is important, too, to Freddy the Pig, though Freddy, being more gregarious, has many friends whose company he enjoys, while Frog and Toad have only each other. And unlike Toad, Freddy does not mind being alone. A good thing, too, for being a writer, he often is (when he can stay awake long enough to enjoy his creative solitude, that is).

For Frog and Toad, friendship is manifested in simply being together—with the added physical fillip of occasionally having their arms unselfconsciously around each other (like small children).

For Freddy, though, friendship is a more active state—friendship is doing, friendship is *helping*! It is Freddy's recognition of a friend's need for his help that is the catalyst for action in most of his adventures. Consider these two examples:

"But this was [Freddy's] friend. She needed his help.

"'All right,' he said. 'I'll do it'" (*Freddy and the Baseball Team from Mars*, 1955, p. 74).

or:

"Oh dear, [Freddy thought]). He'll make me stop defending the sheriff, and I just can't do that. The sheriff's my friend" (*Bean Home News*, p. 113).

C. S. Lewis refines this point a bit: "The mark of perfect friendship is not that help will be given (of course it will) but that, having been given, it makes no difference at all."

"Friendship," Lewis also notes, "must be about something."[37]

In the Frog and Toad books it is about being together.

In strong, idiosyncratic families like Eleanor Estes's Moffats or Betsy Byars's Blossoms, friendship may be about maturation, about a child's breaking out of the family "shell," about establishing his or her individual identity through making a friend of his or her own, as happens with Jane Moffat and Vern Blossom.

Lewis's view is more literal, however. He explains thus: "Friendship arises out of 'mere' companionship when two or more of the companions discover that they have in common some insight or interest or even taste which the others do not share. . . ."[38]

One thing Frog and Toad share is a love of books and reading (a love shared by Freddy the Pig); another is the sharing of stories. Toad is shown reading to Frog on the cover of *Frog and Toad Are Friends*, while one or both can be seen reading on the Table of Contents pages of that book and two of the other titles. I suspect that Lobel is also using these images to echo the I Can Read series title.

C. S. Lewis and the circle of his friends called "The Inklings" also loved reading stories (usually works-in-progress) aloud to each other. Lobel himself loved books and celebrated their therapeutic value. "When I am brought low by the vicissitudes of life, I stumble to my bookshelves. . . . I always feel much better."[39]

Like other children, Frog and Toad also enjoy sharing the experience of being scared. In "Shivers" (*Days*) Frog tells Toad a scary story about the Old Dark Frog. Outside, "The night was cold and dark" (p. 28). But inside, the two friends sit in cozy security in front of the warmth and light of a good fire. "They were having the shivers. It was a good warm feeling" (p. 41). (Beverly

Cleary's everychild, Ramona Quimby, not surprisingly also likes being scared: ". . . she liked the shivery feeling of being scared herself" [*Ramona the Pest*, 1968, p. 129].)

This "good warm feeling" is what Frog and Toad share in story after story, augmented, of course, by the tangible pleasures of hearth and home and good food and drink. (Frog makes a fresh pot of tea before he begins his scary story, for example.)

These sharing experiences are the kinds of "Golden Sessions" that C. S. Lewis celebrates when he rhapsodizes about those times "when four or five of us after a hard day's walking have come to our inn; when our slippers are on, our feet are spread out towards the blaze and our drinks are at our elbows."[40]

Such clubby conviviality, the company of friends enjoying being together in front of a cheery fire at the end of a hard day or of a harrowing adventure, is a regular feature too of the Dolittle books (especially *Gub Gub's Book*) and of the Freddy books.

Home is where the hearth is. But what shines brighter than any fire there is the friendship of Frog and Toad. For wherever they are together is home, where the *heart* is. It is perhaps unconsciously but satisfyingly symbolic that at the end of the final Frog and Toad story, the friends are not seated comfortably in front of a fire with teacups in hand; they are seated together, instead, outdoors on an island with their arms around each other.

No man is an island. But two small animals (universal, surrogate children) *are*—when they are alone . . . together in "immense solitude."

Notes

Robert Lawson

[1]Inman, Sue Lile, "Robert Lawson," in *Dictionary of Literary Biography*, vol. 22, edited by John Cech. Detroit: Gale Research Company, 1983, p. 232.

[2]Lawson, Marie A., "Master of Rabbit Hill—Robert Lawson," in *Newbery Medal Books: 1922–1955*, edited by Bertha Mahony Miller and Elinor Whitney Field. Boston: The Horn Book, Inc., 1955, p. 258.

[3]Lawson, Marie A., p. 259.

[4]Lawson, Marie A., p. 259.

[5]Lawson, Robert, *At That Time*. New York: The Viking Press, 1947, p. 14.

[6]Jones, Helen L., *Robert Lawson, Illustrator*. Boston: Little, Brown and Co., 1972, p. 2.

[7]Jones, p. 22.

[8]Jones, p. 52.

[9]Bader, Barbara, *American Picturebooks from Noah's Ark to the Beast Within*. New York: Macmillan Publishing Co., Inc., 1976, p. 147.

[10]Inman, p. 233.

[11]Jones, p. 73.

[12]Inman, p. 233.

[13]Jones, p. 72.

[14]Jones, p. 81.

[15]Jones, p. 81.

[16]Inman, p. 234.

[17]Lawson, Robert, "Acceptance Paper," in *Newbery Medal Books: 1922–1955*, p. 265.

[18]Blishen, Edward, *Hugh Lofting (Three Bodley Head Monographs)*. London: The Bodley Head, 1968, p. 39.

[19]Watson, Ernest W., *Forty Illustrators*. Freeport, N.Y.: Books for Libraries Press, 1970, p. 190.

[20]Lawson, Robert, "Make Me a Child Again," in *Something Shared: Children and Books*, edited by Phyllis Fenner. New York: The John Day Company, 1959, p. 45.

[21]Lawson, Robert, "Make Me a Child," pp. 50, 53.

[22]Lawson, Robert, "Make Me a Child," p. 46.

[23]Fish, Helen Dean, "Robert Lawson—Illustrator in the Great Tradition," in *Caldecott Medal Books: 1938–1957*, edited by Bertha Mahony Miller and Elinor Whitney Field. Boston: The Horn Book, Inc., 1957, p. 75.

Arnold Lobel

[24]Shannon, George, *Arnold Lobel*. Boston: Twayne Publishers, 1989, p. 99.

[25]Natov, Roni, and Geraldine DeLuca, "An Interview with Arnold Lobel." *The Lion and the Unicorn*, 1:72–96, 1977, p. 80.

[26]Natov, pp. 80–81.

[27]Natov, p. 74.

[28]Lawson, Robert, "Make Me a Child,", pp. 52–53.

[29]"Walter R. Brooks." Knopf promotional brochure, n.d. (ca. 1945), p. 4.

[30]Natov, p. 84.

[31]Natov, p. 88.

[32]Lewis, C. S., *The Four Loves*. New York: Harcourt, Brace and Co., 1960, p. 97.

[33]Natov, p. 77.

[34]Natov, p. 84.

[35]Lobel, Arnold, "A Good Picture Book Should . . ." in *Celebrating Children's Books*, edited by Betsy Hearne and Marilyn Kaye. New York: Lothrop, Lee & Shepard Books, 1981, p. 76.

[36]Lobel, p. 76.
[37]Lewis, p. 102.
[38]Lewis, p. 96.
[39]Lobel, p. 102.
[40]Lewis, p. 105.

Chapter Five

TALLING THE TALE

*"Tall stories are commonly regarded as the
rockbed of American humor. . . ."*
—*E. B. White*, A Subtreasury of American Humor

Bigger Is Better—Paul Bunyan and Pecos Bill

Like Doctor Dolittle before them, Frog and Toad are citizens of
the world. Though they are not globetrotters like the Doctor,
whom we might find anywhere, the garden world they inhabit
is so nonspecific in the details of its setting that *it* could be anywhere . . . or anywhen. As Arnold Lobel has pointed out, "Frog
and Toad belong to no one but they belong to everyone."[1] The
humor that enlivens their adventures is, thus, less specifically
"American" than that of the Lawson animal "biographies" or
of the Freddy books. We have seen in Lawson and Brooks elements of a native American humor, including the lampooning of
authority, the enlivening of conversation with regional simile and

metaphor, and the employing of comically exaggerated regional traits (Yankee taciturnity) to define character. Yet none of these devices is *uniquely* American. To find one that is we need to turn back to the early 1830s, when American humor first became, as Walter Blair puts it, a "graspable phenomenon."[2]

It was, in fact, a British observer who did the grasping. "H.W.," writing in the December 1838 issue of *The London and Westminster Review*, dryly noted, "The curiosity of the public regarding the peculiar nature of American humor seems to have been easily satisfied with the application of the all-sufficing word *exaggeration*" [emphasis added].[3]

A later (American) observer, Constance Rourke, agrees: "extravagance has been a major element in all American comedy."[4]

This major element began to find its expression in the movement of the American frontier away from the Eastern Seaboard into the inland wilderness. For the new land was vast, unexplored and untamed, dwarfing the newcomers, threatening to overwhelm them with the very extravagance of *its* scale. How to deal with it? By matching its natural extravagance with the contrived extravagance of the oral yarns the pioneers began telling around lonely campfires and, later, on the rivers, canals, corduroy roads, and other arteries that pumped life into the wilderness.

"There was a predominance of discomfort and unpleasantness," David B. Kesterson writes with splendid understatement of life on the frontier, "and humor usually derives from adversity of some sort."[5]

The adversity was awesome and the humor it inspired was tall. Alvin Schwartz: "The tall tales which so amuse us spring from the vastness of a frontier wilderness where life was brutal and the people diminished and fearful. They created incredible lies in which individuals were larger and taller than life and could not fail, no matter what."[6]

Sid Fleischman: "It was no accident that the tall tale flourished on the frontier. . . . In laughter, pioneers found a way of accommodating themselves to the agonies that came with the land. Bitter cold? Even words froze in the air. Blowtorch summers? Chickens laid hard-boiled eggs. Raging winds? To pluck a chicken, hold it out the window."[7]

At first, the heroes of the tall tales were real men like Davy Crockett of west Tennessee and Mike Fink of Pennsylvania. It wasn't until decades later that the mythical or literary heroes—Paul Bunyan, Pecos Bill, Febold Feboldson, Joe Magarac, and others—came into being.

At first the stories about Crockett and Fink were spread locally by word of mouth. But by the late 1820s newspapers were becoming a fixture of the frontier, and at the same time there emerged "an intense interest on the part of Americans in things peculiarly American."[8]

The newspapers capitalized on this interest and began printing the stories, thereby assuring a national audience for what had been "peculiarly American" localized tales. The transformation of local, oral tales into a national literature was further enhanced by the election of Davy Crockett to Congress in 1828.

As they would be for Abraham Lincoln several generations later, tall tales and yarns were an important part of Crockett's electioneering: "he would relax his listeners with a good yarn, capture their attention and sometimes apply the moral of his tale to the political issue at hand."[9] Many of these yarns were gathered into a book that "solidified Crockett's reputation as a character and an 'original.'"[10] *The Life and Adventures of Colonel David Crockett of West Tennessee* was published in Cincinnati in 1833 and reprinted the same year in New York under the title *Sketches and Eccentricities of Colonel David Crockett of West Tennessee.* The fame of the man with the coonskin cap was further spread by the publication of his *Autobiography* in 1834 and by a series of *Crockett Almanacs*, which were published annually from 1835 to 1856. Finally, though it might not have seemed so jolly at the time, he had what in retrospect might be called the "good fortune" to be killed at the siege of the Alamo, earning thereby an undying place in American popular myth, folklore, and Walt Disney movies. . . . Indeed, only three years after Crockett's death, an English traveler, Capt. R.C.A. Levinge, wrote of his 1839 trip to Louisville, Kentucky:

"Everything here is Davy Crockett. He was a member of Congress. His voice was so rough it could not be described—it was obliged to be drawn as a picture . . . he picked his teeth with a pitchfork—combed his hair with a rake—fanned himself with a hurricane—He could whip his weight in wildcats—drink the Mississippi dry—he could jump higher, dive deeper, and come up dryer than anyone else . . . he could slide down the slippery end of a rainbow and was half-horse, half-alligator and a bit of snapping turtle."[11]

Similar stories about the legendary keelboatman Mike Fink began appearing in 1828. "Although he died twelve or thirteen years before Crockett, Fink's apotheosis coincides closely with Davy's and they were coupled together in comic fictions."[12]

Though inarguably larger than life, Mike Fink seems never to have reached the nearly demigod status that was ultimately accorded Davy Crockett. Consider the Crockett story that Constance Rourke quotes, about the day it was so cold that the earth froze on its axis and "the sun had got jammed between two cakes o' ice under the wheels. . . . C-R-E-A-T-I-O-N! thought I. . . .

Somethin' must be done, or human creation is done for."

Needless to say, Davy does that "somethin'" and then, Prometheus-like, walks home "introducin' people to the fresh daylight with a piece of sunrise in my pocket."[13]

(Interestingly enough, Doctor Dolittle often attains a similar demigod status in his own discovery and taming of new frontiers; indeed, in one story, by bringing fire to the natives he even becomes, like Davy, a Prometheus figure.)

The American frontier was populated, of course, not only by humans but by animals, some of which, in their turn, attained larger-than-life, tall-tale (or tail!) status. The first and still best-known of these was "The Big Bear of Arkansas," a story that was published in 1841 (and that may have inspired William Faulkner's much later story "The Bear"). How big was he? "'Stranger,' said the man of Arkansaw, ''twould astonish you to know how big he was: I made a bed-spread of his skin, and the way it used to cover my mattress, and leave several feet on each side to tuck up, would have delighted you. It was in fact a creation bar, and if it had lived in Samson's time, and had met him in a fair fight, it would have licked him in the twinkling of a dice box.'"[14]

To tame such animal terrors and magnify their own awesome stature in the bargain, Crockett, Fink, and others gradually began to assume the physical characteristics—teeth, tail, and all—of the threatening animals. As time went by, to meet them was to meet a creature who was half man and half animal. Here is how Crockett and Fink braggingly introduced themselves:

"I'm that same David Crockett, fresh from the backwoods, half-horse, half-alligator, a little touched with the snapping turtle. . . ." (This often-quoted boast originated in *Sketches and Eccentricities of Colonel David Crockett of West Tennessee.*)

Mike Fink asserts, "I'm a Salt River roarer! I'm a ring-tailed squealer! . . . I'm half wild horse and half cock-eyed alligator and the rest of me is crooked snags an' red-hot snappin' turkle!"[15]

Folklorists will point out differences among the brag, the boast, the lie, the whopper, and the tall tale, but to the average reader the important element of commonality is that all play with the truth, and all are informed and infected by exaggeration, extravagance, and stretching of fact. Davy Crockett, Mike Fink, Johnny Appleseed, and—later—John Henry and Casey Jones *were* real people. The woods *were* filled with wild animals, the rivers with alligators, snapping "turkles," and snags. But telling about them, and retelling about them, writing about them and rewriting about them over a procession of years, gradually invested them first with larger-than-life and then later with gargantuan qualities. In their "boastful grandiloquence," stories about them become "tales as big as the continent."[16]

There were more changes to come, however. The early tall-tale heroes were glorifications of regional types—the frontiersman, the Midwest river man, the Kentuckian, and others. The Industrial Revolution of the mid-nineteenth century introduced a new twist in the character of the work giant, the hero who, in his vast size and strength, epitomizes an entire industry: Paul Bunyan, the logging industry; Joe Magarac, the steel industry; Febold Feboldson, agriculture. . . .

In their demystification of the American frontier, the Industrial Revolution and its machines, some feel, destroyed authentic folklore. B. A. Botkin disagrees, pointing out that "The industrial folk tales and songs . . . are evidence enough that machinery does not destroy folklore . . ." and "When the heroes of history go, the demigods arrive. As the ring-tailed roarer is a comic vision of the frontiersman who wrestles single-handed with the wilderness, so our tinkering demigods are the comic culture heroes of an industrial civilization who account for its wonders."[17]

In other words, the natural wonders of the frontier and the wilderness were gradually replaced by mechanical marvels and men—or, more likely, demigods—large enough to match them. Add to this industrialization of America the nation's emergence on the international stage as a participant in World War I, and you lay the groundwork for both a rebirth of the American spirit and a rebirth, in the late 1910s, 1920s, and 1930s, of the tall tale in a new "literary" form and featuring, in the generic personage of the work giant, a host of even *larger* larger-than-life heroes, true demigods like Paul Bunyan, Pecos Bill, Joe Magarac, and Febold Feboldson. Ironically the midwife assisting at the birth of these heroes was modern American commercial advertising, which may be the most direct extant descendant of the frontier tall tale! Paul Bunyan, for example, owes his first fame to a series of pamphlets written about him beginning in 1914 by James Laughead, advertising manager of the Red River Lumber Company in Minneapolis.

Not surprisingly, serious folklorists take exception to the "authenticity" of these new heroes. Richard M. Dorson, for example, grumps, "These figures were created out of whole cloth by writers and promoters in the process I have called 'fakelore,' since they never entered into oral traditions either before or after the publication of their deeds."[18]

Ironically, however, it is this "fakelore" that provides the most enduringly enjoyable humorous experiences for the reader. The original oral tales (and even many of the mid-nineteenth-century written versions) are not so much whoppers as yawners, being in form slight, episodic, anecdotal, allusive and, to modern readers, quaint at best. E. B. White accurately asserts in the introduction to his now-classic *Subtreasury of American Humor*, "Tall stories are commonly regarded as the rockbed of American humor . . . however . . . tall stories can be unspeakably boring. It is possible to be quite tall without being a bit funny."[19]

One example of the dreariness of some authentic folklore will suffice: "Well, I never heard of Paul Bunyan much, but I knowed his daughter. One time she carried a feather tick full of buckshot down the main street of Chippenay Falls and went through the board sidewalk up to her knees every step she took." Richard Dorson, who has quoted this story, observes, "This has the characteristic ring of the few oral stories we can authenticate: brief, sidelong tall-tale capsules."[20]

Happily such "capsules" were enough to fire the imaginations of more literary sensibilities. The same decade that saw the publication of *The Story of Doctor Dolittle* and *To and Again* saw the publication of the first modern, imaginative collection of tall-tale stories: Esther Shephard's *Paul Bunyan*, which was published in 1924 with suitably heroic illustrations by Rockwell Kent. While Shephard's version (and the other "hero" stories that had preceded it in print in the nineteenth century) was not published for children, young readers quickly adopted it. And why not? The comic, larger-than-life qualities of the tall tale are irresistible to young readers. Child psychologist Martha Wolfenstein points out the "predicament of children in relation to adults . . . their longing to be big and . . . how they express these [longings] in the funny stories they invent . . . the admired and envied size of the adults is exaggerated so that it becomes grotesque. . . ."[21]

It is equally irresistible to strike an analogy between the children's envy of adults' size and the presumed need of pioneers—reduced to the size of children by the vastness of the wilderness—to express their needs in the creation of stories about giants (i.e., adults). One presumes that nineteenth-century children were equally fascinated with the tall tales that circulated then, particularly because of children's perverse fascination with the usually violent nature of their themes and contents. As for tall tales created specifically *for* children, critic Sheila Egoff finds "the first of the 'tall tales' which were to become such a strong part of American children's literature" not in stories of frontier heroes but rather in Frank R. Stockton's whimsical *The Casting Away of Mrs. Lecks and Mrs. Aleshine* (1886).[22] (Some readers might think that *Tom Sawyer* and *Huckleberry Finn* are the more logical choices [both preceded the Stockton title—*Tom* by ten years and *Huck* by one]. Certainly there is no question that their author, Mark Twain, had been heavily influenced by the humor of the old Southwest, which gave rise to the traditions of tall-tale humor.)

In the twentieth century a second collection of Paul Bunyan tales, Glen Rounds's delightful *Ol' Paul, The Mighty Logger* (1936), *was* clearly written for children. Though simpler in style than Shephard's earlier version, the Rounds version too respects the classic form of the tall tale. Both, for example, are first-person narratives by loggers who claim to have known Ol' Paul and to have worked for him on the Big Onion and elsewhere. Both versions present even the most outlandish incidents with a straight face and avowals of their truth. To reinforce *their* truthfulness, the respective narrators often disallow the truth of earlier versions. Glen Rounds, for example, decries the story that Paul "kept his great beard in a buckskin bag made from the skins of seventy-seven deer and took it out only on odd Sundays and legal holidays to comb it. The truth of the matter is," he continues, "that the bag was made of the skins of one hundred and sixteen elk, and he wore it only at night, to keep catamounts and such from bedding down in his whiskers" (pp. 9–10).

Both narrators also provide great detail to support the

veracity of their stories. Babe, Paul's giant blue ox, for example, is not just forty-two ax handles between the eyes but forty-two ax handles and a tobacco box (!), according to Shephard (p. xii). Such details, of course, vary with the teller (as the old-timer on the *Fibber McGee and Molly* radio show might have put it, "That ain't the way I heerd it!"). Thus, Rounds asserts that Babe's between-the-eyes measurement was one hundred and seventy-one ax handles, three small cans of tomatoes, and a plug of chewing tobacco laid end to end (p. 11).

If the original tall tales were created with a purpose—the taming of the wild frontier with the humor of exaggeration—and were rooted in real people and a real landscape, exaggerated for comedic purpose, these later tall tales seem to exist largely for the purpose of expanding the frontier of the imagination. A kind of "can you top this" mentality takes over, and stories assume an increasing overlay of fantasy. This is not confined to the Paul Bunyan stories. Consider those about the second great American hero to make his first in-print appearance in the 1920s: Pecos Bill, "the greatest cowboy of all time," as James Cloyd Bowman has described him. Bill was "born" in the pages of the October 1923 *Century Magazine* in a story called "The Saga of Pecos Bill" by Edward J. "Tex" O'Reilly. As was the case with Paul Bunyan, a sedate debate continues to simmer as to the "authenticity" of Bill as a genuine folk hero. Shephard and another teller of Bunyan tales, James Stevens, claim to have actually interviewed lumberjacks who heard and told stories about the mighty logger around logging campfires. Similarly, Bowman, who wrote the first book for children about Pecos Bill's legendary exploits, has this to say: "During the last three decades of the nineteenth century our civilization opened two new frontiers and added two new heroes of gargantuan proportions [Paul Bunyan and Pecos Bill]." He goes on to assert, of the material in his book *Pecos Bill* (1937), "This is a volume of genuine American folklore," adding, rather breathlessly, "These adventures . . . constitute a part of the Saga of the Cowboy. They are collected from the annals of the campfire and the roundup" (p. 7).

Whether the stories of Pecos Bill are fakelore or folklore is moot and probably of little interest to the average reader. The point is that, like those of Paul Bunyan, they delight the imagination and tickle the funnybone in their extravagance and fantastic wit.

Pecos Bill may, in fact, be a bit closer to the original heroes—Davy Crockett and Mike Fink among them—than Ol' Paul, at least in his beginnings, which borrow the tradition of the half-man, half-animal nature of the hero and take it one step further: He is actually raised by coyotes, who name him "Cropear." Discovered by a wandering cowboy, Bill is finally convinced of his human identity by being shown his reflection in a pool of water. In Bowman's version the cowboy turns out to be Bill's brother, who quickly recognizes Bill's unusual . . . *potential*: "By the little roan bull's bellow, you're as perfect as old Davy Crockett, and the world will bear me out in that statement as soon as she's been properly introduced" (p. 42).

In fact Bill, in the prodigiousness of his deeds, will out-Crockett Crockett. For starters, of course, he "invents" modern cowpunching, just as Paul Bunyan had "invented" logging. Thereafter the thematic similarities of the Bill and Bunyan stories strongly support Bowman's claim that the two were "blood brothers."

For starters the natural world that they inhabit is informed by a similarly bizarre topography (in the literary tall tale, setting, like character, evolves from broad exaggeration to fantasy): Paul starts a logging camp at the Pyramid Forty, a mountain so high that it takes a man a week to see to its top, while Bill starts the Perpetual Motion Ranch on Pinnacle Mountain, which was "round as a silver dollar at the base" and rose "ten or a dozen thousand feet above the clouds to a point so sharp an eagle couldn't hardly keep his balance on it" (p. 83). Of course, the animals that live on the Pyramid and on Pinnacle Mountain, respectively, have adapted to their vertical environment: Their "inside" legs are shorter than their "outside" legs, while the birds that nest there lay square eggs (round ones would roll down the mountainside, of course). If *this* sounds like "eggsaggeration" (though not without logic in the adaptation of fauna to an . . . unusual environment), other animals are even more fantastic (exaggeration giving way to fantasy again). There is the wouser in the Pecos Bill stories: A cross between the mountain lion and the grizzly bear, it is "ten times larger than either. Besides that," Bowman tells us, "he was the nastiest creature in the world" (p. 19). Or how about the hodag, which is a fauna fixture of the Bunyan yarns: Aside from making an awful noise—"the worst you ever heard" according to Shephard (p. 30)—"he wasn't pretty to look at neither—especially if you was by yourself . . ." unless you happen to think a creature with horns on the back of its legs like a rooster's, only twelve hundred times as big, and long claws and big spikes all along its back and stiff hair all over its body that burns you like nettles when you get close to it is pretty, that is. . . .

The weather is often as ugly as a hodag. Paul is plagued by winters so cold that the snow turns blue. Bill has to deal with droughts: He digs a canal and then, to keep it filled with water, has to lasso a ten-mile stretch of the Rio Grande each day. "Every morning before breakfast Bill had to rope himself another length"

(p. 218). Or there was the time when it began raining *up* at Bunyan's lumber camp and Paul had to disguise himself as a rainstorm to find out why. Bill, meanwhile, is busy riding a cyclone to earth like a bucking bronco; the force with which he comes to ground—in California—is so great that it creates Death Valley. Of course, that's nothing compared to Paul's inadvertent creation of the Grand Canyon by thoughtlessly dragging his pickax behind him. Perhaps it is inevitable that in some versions Paul and Bill actually meet up, as when Bill teaches Paul how to ride a thunderbolt.

For it is a natural world of wonders these two giants inhabit, a vivid demonstration that in America bigger may not necessarily be better, but it is indubitably . . . bigger. Together Bill and Bunyan trimmed it down to size and left it a little tamer than they found it. The civilization that inevitably followed saw the end of the physical presences of the two demigods, but the spirit of their larger-than-life, exaggerated, and extravagant personalities and adventures lives on not only in the splendid stories about them that survive but in the influence they visited on the work of the authors and illustrators who would come after them. New versions of the tall-tale canon continue to appear regularly. For only one example: The popular artist-author Steven Kellogg has recently completed a memorable quartet of new versions of stories about Bill, Bunyan, Mike Fink, and Johnny Appleseed. The exuberance of Kellogg's artistic style and the broad exaggeration of his visual humor are perfect complements to the extravagance of the stories. Other authors, while not writing new versions of established tall tales have, nevertheless been influenced by their tone, form, and conventions. Two of the most notable of these authors are Robert McCloskey and Sid Fleischman.

Robert McCloskey

"So you never can tell what will happen when you learn to play the harmonica." — Lentil *by Robert McCloskey*

It was appropriate that the first book Robert McCloskey would illustrate but not write was a collection of tall tales: Anne Malcolmson's now-classic collection *Yankee Doodle's Cousins* (1941). McCloskey, in his own first book, *Lentil* (1940), had already demonstrated his creative debt to the tone and spirit of traditional American humor and its tall tales. His biographer, Gary D. Schmidt, notes, "*Lentil* is a tall tale in the American tradition of tall tales."[23] As evidence he cites its exaggerations, its straight-faced narrative tone, and its episodic nature. To this he might also have added its protagonist. Granted, as Schmidt notes, Lentil "is not Pecos Bill or John Henry or Stormalong." But it does seem that he is their equal, if not in physical size, then certainly in his imperturbable wit, enterprise, and ingenuity. The resolution of the problem is his invention. And it is every bit as delightful to the reader as any number of viewings of the skin of the Big Bear of Arkansas!

McCloskey was born in 1914 in Hamilton, Ohio, which would provide the small-town setting for not only *Lentil* but also his two books for older readers, *Homer Price* (1943) and its sequel, *Centerburg Tales* (1951). He was educated at the Vesper George School of Art in Boston and the National Academy of Design in New York.

"I was studying to be an artist," he recalled in his first Caldecott Medal acceptance speech, "and I was hell-bent on creating *art*. My mind in those days was filled with odd bits of Greek mythology, with accent on Pegasus, Spanish galleons, Oriental dragons, and all the stuff that really and truly great art is made of. . . . It was at this time [1935] that I made my first visit to New York. . . . I went to call on an editor of children's books. . . . she looked at the examples of great art I had brought along. . . . I don't remember *just* the words she used to tell me to get wise to myself and shelve the dragons, Pegasus, limpid pool business, and learn how and what to 'art' with. . . . I went back to Boston a very puzzled art student."[24]

The editor was the great May Massee, children's book editor of The Viking Press (and also Robert Lawson's editor). Her advice took, and McCloskey quickly realized that what he had to "art" with were the remembered small-town scenes of his childhood in Hamilton. Three years later, in 1938, he returned to New York and May Massee's office with a book dummy to show her.

"I looked at it," Miss Massee later recalled, "and was crazy about it. . . . And [McCloskey] said, 'You like it?' I said, 'Yes, I like it very much.' He said, 'You're really going to publish it?' 'Yes,' I said, 'We're really going to publish it. . . .'"[25]

The dummy was, of course, for *Lentil*, which *was* published in 1940.

The eponymous hero, Lentil, is a young, barefoot boy whose principal problem in life is that he cannot sing ("When he opened his mouth to try, only strange sounds came out . . .") and he can't even whistle because he can't pucker his lips. "But he did want to make music, so he saved up enough pennies to buy a harmonica." Determined to become an expert, "he played a lot, whenever and whatever he could. His favorite place to practice was in the bathtub, because there the tone was improved one hundred per cent." Everybody in Alto, Lentil's hometown, likes his music except for one old crab, Old Sneep, who doesn't like much of anything—or anybody, not even the great Colonel Carter, who has donated such civic fixtures as the public library, Carter Memorial Park, and the Soldiers and Sailors Monument. When news arrives that the Colonel is returning to Alto after a two-year absence, Old Sneep grouches, "Humph! . . . He ain't a mite better'n you or me and he needs takin' down a peg or two."

The way Old Sneep contrives to do this is . . . *deliciously* outlandish. In good American fashion, a brass band is assembled to serenade the arrival, by train, of the Colonel. The whole town, led by its mayor (who is anxious, no doubt, to give a speech), turns out at the train station.

"The train pulled in. The musicians in the band were waiting for the leader to signal them to play, the leader was waiting for the mayor to nod to him to start the band, and the mayor was waiting for Colonel Carter to step from his private car. All the people held their breath and waited.

"Then there was a wet sound from above. There sat Old Sneep [on the roof of the train depot], sucking on a lemon."

Well, the musicians' lips pucker so they can't play, and it appears that all will be lost. But, of course, Lentil's lips aren't puckered (he *can't* pucker his lips, remember?), and so, enterprisingly, he takes out his harmonica and plays—not something dignified or fancy but a rousing version of a good, old-fashioned American tune, "Comin' Round the Mountain When She Comes."

The day is saved! The Colonel (who looks a *lot* like Daddy Warbucks with pupils) is delighted; in fact, he proves—even though a wealthy mover and shaker—to be such a regular fellow that he takes over the harmonica playing when Lentil's wind gives out, stopping only long enough to announce that he is going to build a new hospital for the town. "So," McCloskey concludes, "you never can tell what will happen when you learn to play the harmonica."

What happened to McCloskey was that he turned into one of America's greatest creators of books for children. For make no mistake, Lentil is McCloskey as a boy. Not only did McCloskey grow up in a small town just like Alto, but he was a harmonica player too—even practicing in his own bathtub, as Lentil would do later. In looking at McCloskey's three "Ohio" books—*Lentil*, *Homer Price*, and *Centurburg Tales*—it is hard to disagree with Helen W. Painter's sweeping assertion, "Perhaps seldom has an individual in his representation of reality verging on the comic made greater use of his own background and personal characteristics in his work than has Robert McCloskey."[26]

McCloskey himself admitted as much, though adding, perhaps wistfully, "I wish I had been barefoot more of the time."[27]

The Alto of *Lentil* could also stand as the portrait in words and pictures of the quintessential American small town of the same American moment—the 1920s and early 1930s—when the literary tall tale was flourishing. May Hill Arbuthnot called it "a juvenile *Main Street*,"[28] though the element of satire that McCloskey brings to his portrait is much gentler than Sinclair Lewis brought to his depiction of Gopher Prairie.

Anyone who grew up in an American small town will recognize the authenticity of Alto as it is lovingly depicted on the book's marvelous endpapers. There is the obligatory river, spanned by both a covered bridge and a steel railroad bridge. There is an elaborate depot toward which steams a passenger train pulled by a coal-burning locomotive. There is the town park in whose very center stands a soldiers and sailors monument. There are the churches, the wooden frame buildings (some of which, the text of the book will tell us, are a public library, a drugstore, and a barber shop), and the vehicles—the cars, the truck, and even a horse-drawn wagon. Farms encroach on the town, and there are, of course, trees everywhere (one almost expects to see Johnny Apple-seed vanishing over a distant hill). Indeed, it is the setting, as well as the story, that validates Dora V. Smith's description of the book as being "as authentic Americana as it is good humor."[29]

In his use of Americana, McCloskey was reflecting not only his own background and upbringing but also a prevailing motif in the American art of the day. As he recalls, "in the thirties in the Depression days, Americana was the big theme of American art; we were just beginning to discover ourselves. . . ."[30]

As *Lentil* demonstrated, for McCloskey that phrase "discover ourselves" meant discovering our past. It clearly meant the same thing for his contemporary Robert Lawson; the same year *Lentil* appeared, Lawson's loving tribute to his American ancestors, *They Were Strong and Good* (1940), won the Caldecott Medal. While Lawson was busy discovering his ancestors, McCloskey was engaged in discovering his art; and *his* next book for Viking, *Make Way for Ducklings*, by winning the coveted Caldecott Medal, proved that he found it.

McCloskey was also discovering himself as a writer—though not necessarily by choice. As he told Ethel Heins, then editor of *The Horn Book*, "May [Massee] liked my drawings, and she said, 'I haven't anything for you to illustrate . . . why don't you go home and write something?'"[31] What he wrote when he got home was *Homer Price*, which Ms. Heins, four decades later, called "Mark Twain almost reconstituted."[32]

"For contemporary reviewers," Schmidt adds, "*Homer Price* was [McCloskey's] most American book."[33] Indeed, *The Saturday Review* enthused that "No country on earth but the United States could have produced Homer Price and his fellow citizens."[34]

James Daugherty, writing in *The Horn Book*, said of *Homer Price*, "It is America laughing at itself with a broad and genial humanity. . . . It is the true comedy of democracy. . . ."[35]

Incidentally, the publication of this and a similarly laudatory companion piece by architect Eric Gugler was orchestrated by May Massee herself, according to Schmidt. Massee magisterially dismissed *Horn Book* editor Bertha Mahoney Miller's plan to ask Walter R. Brooks (!) to write this piece by announcing, "I like Walter R. Brooks and I like his books, but the older I get the more I realize authors just simply can't review each other's books, especially when they are in the same genre."[36] This seems disingenuous at best, since Massee then took it upon herself to ask one of her Viking authors (James Daugherty) and the architect (Gugler) who had designed her office at Viking to write the pieces and apparently to submit them to her for her review before she passed them on to *The Horn Book* for publication!

Ethical considerations aside, a certain latitude for flag-waving exaggeration should be granted to contemporary reviewers, since *Homer Price*, it must be remembered, appeared in 1943, in the middle of World War II (or, as friend of mine who served in the military at that time was fond of calling it, "the *big* war." A certain American hyperbole creeps into our reminiscence as well as our literature . . .).

Yet even with the distance of the fifty-plus years that have passed since *Homer* first appeared, it must be admitted that in terms of its characters, setting, and tone, and the tall-tale humor that leavens its plots (it is, after all, not a novel but an interrelated series of six short stories), *Homer Price* is a quintessentially American book.

Its setting, the town of Centerburg, is, of course, Alto updated by the passage of a couple of decades of "progress." The new name, Centerburg, is a nice touch, evoking the quintessentially American "booster" mentality that infected founding fathers across the length and breadth of the U.S. of A., who were convinced that each hamlet and village that they founded was, perforce, the very center of the American universe (the village that provides the setting for the action of many of the Freddy the Pig books is, of course, Center*boro*).

The book's protagonist, Homer Price, is still Lentil but a more worldly version—he's put away his harmonica and put on a pair of shoes. The other characters who populate Homer's hometown are classic American comic types: There is Homer's uncle Ulysses, the typical booster who owns a "very up and coming lunch room" and is a true believer in progress as it is epitomized in labor-saving devices. There is the sheriff, a spoonerism-spouting political hack who is too busy getting his hair cut and talking about the World Series to help Homer capture a band of gun-toting bandits. There is the Judge, a pompous blowhard whose pronouncements are delivered in capital letters ("'Yep,' said Homer, 'the Judge mentioned that she had come to live in Centerburg. He said that she was a Public Spirited Person, and would be An Addition To The Town'" [p. 127]). And there is the Mayor, who, observing all the children of Centerburg following a reconstituted Pied Piper out of town, can only think to moan: "Sheriff, we can't lose all these children with election time coming up next month" (p.120). These "civic leaders" routinely gather in the barber shop or the lunch room to argue, gossip, and—no doubt—spin the tall tale or three. In the tone of the stories, in the lightly satirical way in which McCloskey presents these characters and their familiar foibles and failings, *Homer Price* recalls many of the popular radio comedies of the 1930s and 1940s that also had small-town settings—most notably the greatest of them all, *Fibber McGee and Molly*. As Walter Blair notes, "Finally an Elysium and an El Dorado for storytellers was a sensationally popular network [radio] show . . . 'Fibber McGee and Molly.' Year after year its scriptwriter Don Quinn populated it with yarnspinners. . . . Chief of the group was . . . Fibber himself, who every Tuesday evening told monstrous untrue tales. . . . And other loquacious tellers of windies joined this star in unwinding yarns. . . ."[37]

Speaking of the radio: Something else of significance has happened that separates Centerburg from Alto, something that is expressed in B. A. Botkin's assertion that "Next to rural brags and gags, the most fertile source of tall tales is industry and remarkable inventions . . . an expression of the mechanical genius of Americans which has flowered in folklore ranging from Yankee contraptions . . . to the large-scale contrivances of Paul Bunyan."[38]

No wonder Homer is a tinkerer whose hobby is building radios. McCloskey played the harmonica as a boy, yes, but he was also crazy about machines, and even in the adult McCloskey, his one-time roommate Marc Simont remembers a "talent for devising mechanical contraptions [which] is topped only by his ability to turn out books that carry off the Caldecott Medal."[39]

Homer's parents operate a tourist camp and filling station, serving the needs of restless Americans traveling on the open road in automobiles; yes, automobiles, that most American of "mechanical contraptions." One almost expects Henry Ford to show up in his Model A and to breezily tell Homer to "fill 'er up." Homer's uncle Ulysses, as previously noted, operates a "very up and coming lunch room over in Centerburg" and is a passionate believer in labor-saving devices, most notably his automatic doughnut machine, which will serve as the catalyst for what is perhaps the most famous of the Homer Price stories.

It is the incongruity of the traditional small-town setting and the inroads of a modern mechanical age (some would call it "progress") that provides much of the humor of the book. Indeed, it reaches its zenith in the final story, the gently satirical "Wheels of Progress," which couples a typical small-town historical pageant—"One Hundred and Fifty Years of Centerburg Progress"—with the dedication of a new suburb, "Enders Heights," which consists of one hundred houses that "looked as alike as a hundred doughnuts." No wonder, since they are all prefabricated according to Uncle Ulysses's theories of progress, Homer's uncle having finally found in the wealthy Miss Enders someone who "was receptive to [his] up and comingness and, what's more, she had the money to be receptive and up and coming *with*" (p. 130).

At first things go fairly well. The houses are built. People move in, and in the absence of street signs—which Dulcey Dooner, the President (and only member) of the Street Sign Putter Uppers Union, refuses to erect unless he's paid ten dollars per installation—the new tenants, with typical American ingenuity, quickly realize that the easiest way to find which one of the hundred identical homesteads is theirs is to count from a landmark: the Enders Homestead, which survives to sit in Victorian splendor right in the middle of the subdivision.

Unfortunately the wealthy Miss Enders has been so captivated by Uncle Ulysses's theories of up and comingness that she begins to feel that "her house seemed out of place." She's not alone: "Uncle Ulysses and the Judge agreed that the Homestead did stand out like a sore thumb" (p. 141). This is funny for the reader for two reasons: First, he or she already knows that *any* idea emanating from these two comically fatuous characters is bound to result in hilarious disorder, and second, this knowledge invokes a sense of pleasurable anticipation of the comicalities to come— the same kind of anticipation with which small children wait for Christmas.

Sure enough, the Judge and Uncle Ulysses decide that the

house must be moved before that evening's pageant. Later, Uncle Ulysses "ironed out his difficulty with Dulcey . . ." (p. 41) (sure he did, the reader thinks with a grin of anticipation), and the pageant begins.

The pageant itself is worthy of comment. To the citizens of Centerburg it is a celebration of the town's, uh, *colorful* past. To readers, however, it is a sly send-up of the American dream, the same kind of send-up found in Meredith Willson's satirical musical comedy *The Music Man*.

Here's the story: Pioneer Ezekiel Enders, "hearing of the fertile lands to the West," sets off for the wilderness with his family snugly ensconced in a covered wagon. Alas, trouble plagues them and finally they find themselves in an inhospitable wilderness "with no food to sustain life" (p. 142). Then a miracle: On the very spot where the pageant is being held, Ezekiel finds "forty-two pounds of edible fungus growing in the forest." The family is saved. A town is born. Time passes. The Enders descendants found a patent-medicine company using Grandpa's formula for a "Cough Syrup and Elixir of Life compound." Peace and prosperity reign. A choir raises its voice in jubilant song:

"Forty-two pounds of edible fungus
   In the wilderness a-growin'
   Saved the settlers from starvation,
   Helped the founding of this nation" (p. 143).

The pageant ends with a torchlight procession to Enders Heights, the tangible expression of Uncle Ulysses's idea of progress, which will, presumably, be the stuff of another pageant 150 years in the future.

But wait! Disorder looms. Where are the street signs? Where is

Dulcey Dooner? Where is the Enders Homestead?

No signs. No Dooner. No Homestead—it's been replaced by another cookie- (or doughnut-) cutter house. Confusion. Consternation. The adults are in an uproar.

Of course, it's up to Homer to save the day.

"It was Homer and [his friend] Freddy . . . who found the little wooden keg near the corner. They smelled it. They tasted it. Freddy shouted, 'I know—it's cough syrup!'

"'And Elixir Compound!' added Homer" (pp. 147–49).

It turns out that old Ezekiel Enders—under siege by the local Indians, who had become addicted to his Elixir—buried his jug of syrup, along with the formula, underneath his cabin, which stood on the *very site* of the recently moved Enders Homestead. Dulcey, digging a hole for a sign post, has discovered it and has taken what Doctor Pelly diagnoses as "an overdose of Cough Syrup and Elixir of Life compound, aged over a hundred years in a wooden keg" (p. 149).

Since Homer and Freddy have established where the Homestead stood, the subdivision tenants can count from that point to find their respective homes.

But no one is taking any chances: The Homestead is quickly moved back to its rightful place in the middle of the subdivision.

This is all the stuff of gentle satire, of course, of poking fun at the silliness of a too-true belief in the "religion" of progress. But it also holds the past up for satirical scrutiny. There is humor there, too, in the distance we discover between historical fact and the embellished version, which imagination, the passage of time, and the American penchant for exaggeration have created.

There's a sweet innocence about all of this—a good-natured skating over the surface of reality. Thinking about it reminds us of Max Eastman's observation: "In everything that we do perceive as funny there is an element which, if we were serious and sufficiently sensitive and sufficiently concerned, would be unpleasant."[40]

McCloskey's tone in "Wheels of Progress" invokes and invites a certain distance from such "seriousness." In the fictions of *Homer Price*, McCloskey the writer could smile at "progress" and poke gentle fun at it. In real life, however, McCloskey the man could be "sufficiently sensitive" and "sufficiently concerned" to see the unpleasantness there. In his second Caldecott Medal Acceptance Speech, McCloskey revealed his anger: "I'm beginning to fear that with our machines, and machine-made materials, we are designing nature right out of our environment." (Miss Enders, gazing out at her newly constructed subdivision, rhapsodizes: "Simply marvelous. . . . Just think. Last week there were only grass and trees and squirrels on this spot!") "In this country," McCloskey continued, "we have been designing, building, making things with machines without paying the vaguest attention to the space around what we've produced. . . . And how do the houses look, lined up row after row, aerial to aerial in the housing development of an unimaginative builder? *They look like hell* [emphasis added]."[41]

If Lentil is McCloskey as a harmonica-playing boy, Homer is—while being himself very much a boy—a surrogate for the adult McCloskey. Homer is skeptical, inventive, ingenious, and brighter than any of the adults who surround him. It is Homer who devises a plan to capture the radio robbers; it is Homer who recognizes that Michael Murphy is not—as the sheriff has self-importantly announced—Rip Van Winkle redux but instead the Pied Piper; and it is Homer who has had the enterprise to get cotton to put in all the children's ears. In *Centerburg Tales*, the sequel to *Homer Price*, it is, once again, Homer who recognizes in Dulcey Dooner's gigantic plants (more tall-tale exaggeration) not exotic flowers but (oh, dear) humble ragweed and, moreover, "doggedly" devises a way to get rid of their seeds (read the story to find out how). It is Homer the skeptic who discovers that the cans of "Ever So Much More So" that all the adults have bought are . . . empty. ("'We've been dindled, doggonit—I mean swindled,' howled the sheriff." [p. 146].) And, of course, it is Homer as reader who remembers a Mark Twain story that provides a cure for the rhyming malady that infects Centerburg in "Pie and Punch and You-Know-Whats."

If Homer's ingenuity and problem-solving prowess elevate him to at least the de facto status of tall-tale hero, McCloskey's own attitude toward the tall-tale genre is personified in the character of Homer's Grampa Hercules, who is a mainstay of *Centerburg Tales* and easily the most sympathetic adult character in either book.

Grampa is an inveterate teller of tall tales and, accordingly, is much loved by Homer and the other Centerburg kids, who clamor, "Tell us a story, Grampa Herc."

Grampa's stories are in the classic tall-tale mode involving natural "wonders" (a "bump" in a creek so high a raft can't float over it); prodigies of strength (lifting a horse: "Wu-a-ll, a horse is a sure enough hard thing to lift. 'Tisn't that he's so heavy, but the critter's feet keep getting in the way. It takes a mighty tall man to walk up to a horse and pick 'im up off the ground"), and marvelous inventions (the "Hide-a-Ride": "I declare, it was the gosh-awfullest-looking contraption I ever did see but, by gorry, it worked!") (pp. 18–22).

The kids adore these stories even though Homer admits that "you know how he is, it's hard to tell when he's telling one of his stories and when he's telling what's really so" (p. 11).

The adults are less forgiving and more stridently skeptical, leading Grampa to observe, "The trouble with you fellas is not enough exercise. You're getting older and losing your sense of humor" (p. 29). Grampa must have known Balzac, who gloomily observed: "As children only do we laugh, and as we travel onward laughter sinks down and dies out like the light of an oil-lit lamp."[42]

Grampa is the only adult who has not lost the ability to laugh, to play with his imagination. Ultimately this will lead him into trouble: He makes the mistake of telling one of his whoppers (about the time he jumped 300 feet) in the presence of two advertising men. Before he knows it, Grampa has been made a partner in the Gabby and Maxwell Container Package and Advertising Company! McCloskey deftly demonstrates here the unhappy truth that the tall-tale mantle in this century has passed from the indigenous storyteller to the world of advertising and marketing. He also makes this point by conjuring up wacky names for breakfast food—"Whoopsy-Doodles," "Wheatsy-Beatsys," and "Vimmy Swimmys"—while Grampa himself has already complained of the problems such inroads visit on storytellers: "A storyteller's got enough trouble on his hands nowadays trying to hold his own against Super-Dupers and rocket ships and all kinds o' newfangled truck" (p. 38). Of course, McCloskey has already made this point for him in *Homer Price*, where we actually meet the Super-Duper (a wickedly funny pastiche of Superman) and find that the superheroes of today's comics, who have replaced the tall-tale heroes of yesterday, have feats of clay. . . .

The trouble with the adults—and with the advertising men—is that they take Grampa's stories literally and demand that they not only make literal sense but also be consistent! With his superior wisdom, Grampa points out, "That story keeps getting older and changing every year, just like people . . . this story keeps getting older and better." It is, in fact, organic, like the traditional tall tale that, passing from teller to teller, grew, expanded, and changed in its details while retaining its elemental truth. When Grampa is put in the awkward position by the advertising men of demonstrating the literal truth of one of the feats that has been the centerpiece of a tall tale, it is, appropriately, the kids who—with *their* untrammeled imaginations—devise a strategy for saving both his face and the spirit of his story.

Grampa's stories, like their tall-tale progenitors, have the power to endure because they celebrate, with imagination and humor, the human capacity to overcome all manner of obstacles and ordeals and to laugh in the process.

Alvin Schwartz, lamenting the diminishing importance of folklore, has observed, "As a result . . . we have to a serious extent become alienated from our traditions and have lost a sense of place and a sense of self."[43]

It is McCloskey's genius to have restored those traditions in the themes and plots of *Lentil*, *Homer Price*, and *Centerburg Tales*, and to have created in their fondly remembered settings a now-long-gone small-town America. And, finally, in the character of Homer Price, with his wit, unflappable panache, ingenuity, and enterprise, to have created a paradigm of the idealized American.

Notes

Paul Bunyan and Pecos Bill

[1] Natov, Roni, and Geraldine DeLuca, "An Interview with Arnold Lobel." *The Lion and the Unicorn*, 1:72–96, 1977, p. 95.

[2] Blair, Walter, *Native American Humor (1800–1900)*. New York: American Book Company, 1937, p. 39.

[3] Quoted in Blair, pp. 138–39.

[4] Rourke, Constance, *American Humor: A Study of the National Character*. New York: Harcourt, Brace and Co., 1931, p. 299.

[5] Kesterson, David B., "West," in *American Humor: A Historical Survey* (*Dictionary of Literary Biography*, vol. 11, part 2), edited by Stanley Trachtenberg. Detroit: Gale Research Company, 1982, p. 620.

[6] Schwartz, Alvin, "Children, Humor, and Folklore, Part II." *The Horn Book*, LIII:474, August 1977.

[7] Fleischman, Sid, "Laughter and Children's Literature." *The Horn Book*, LII:467, October 1976.

[8] Inge, M. Thomas, *The Frontier Humorists*. Hamden, Conn.: Archon Books, 1975, p. 1.

[9] Dorson, Richard M., *America in Legend*. New York: Pantheon Books, 1973, p. 65.

[10] Dorson, p. 65.

[11] Quoted in Dorson, pp. 76–77.

[12] Dorson, p. 92.

[13] Quoted in Rourke, pp. 58–59.

[14] Quoted in Meine, Franklin J., "Tall Tales of the Southwest," in Inge, p. 23.

[15] Botkin, B. A., *A Treasury of American Folklore*. New York: Crown Publishers, 1944, pp. 56–57.

[16] Erdoes, Richard, *Tales from the American Frontier*. New York: Pantheon, 1991, p. xv.

[17]Botkin, pp. xxii, 175.

[18]Dorson, p. 247.

[19]White, E. B., and Katharine S. White, eds., *A Subtreasury of American Humor*. New York: The Modern Library, 1941, p. xvi.

[20]Dorson, p. 170.

[21]Wolfenstein, Martha, *Children's Humor: A Psychological Analysis*. Bloomington: Indiana University Press, 1978, pp. 18–19.

[22]Egoff, Sheila A., *Worlds Within*. Chicago: American Library Association, 1988, p. 70.

Robert McCloskey

[23]Schmidt, Gary D., *Robert McCloskey*. Boston: Twayne Publishers, 1990, p. 23.

[24]McCloskey, Robert, "Ducklings at Home and Abroad," in *Caldecott Medal Books: 1938–1957*, edited by Bertha Mahony Miller and Elinor Whitney Field. Boston: The Horn Book, Inc., 1957, pp. 81–82.

[25]Schmidt, p. 5.

[26]Painter, Helen W., "Robert McCloskey: Master of Humorous Realism," in *Authors and Illustrators of Children's Books*, edited by Miriam Hoffman and Eva Samuels. New York: R. R. Bowker Co., 1972, p. 308.

[27]Schmidt, p. 23.

[28]Arbuthnot, May Hill, *Children and Books*. Chicago: Scott, Foresman and Co., 1947, p. 379.

[29]Smith, Dora V., *Fifty Years of Children's Books*. Champaign, Ill.: National Council of Teachers of English, 1963, p. 51.

[30]Schmidt, p. 7.

[31]"Bothering to Look: A Conversation Between Robert McCloskey and Ethel Heins," in *Innocence and Experience*, edited by Barbara

Harrison and Gregory Maguire. New York: Lothrop, Lee & Shepard Books, 1987, p. 334.

[32] "Bothering," p. 333.

[33] Schmidt, p. 8.

[34] Schmidt, p. 29.

[35] Daugherty, James, "Homer Price: Comment by Eric Gugler and James Daugherty," *The Horn Book*, XIX:426, November 1943.

[36] Schmidt, p. 9.

[37] Blair, Walter, *Tall Tale America*. Chicago: The University of Chicago Press, 1987, p. 263.

[38] Botkin, p. 492.

[39] Simont, Marc, "Bob McCloskey, Inventor," in *Newbery and Caldecott Medal Books: 1956–65*, edited by Lee Kingman. Boston: The Horn Book, Inc., 1965, p. 196.

[40] Eastman, Max, *Enjoyment of Laughter*. New York: Simon & Schuster, 1936, p. 21.

[41] McCloskey, Robert, "Caldecott Award Acceptance," in *Newbery and Caldecott Medal Books: 1956–1965*, p. 192.

[42] Quoted in Eastman, p. 137.

[43] Schwartz, pp. 475–76.

Chapter Six

SID FLEISCHMAN

*"Language is a wondrous toy
and I have great literary fun with it."*
Sid Fleischman—Interview with the author

Thank God for the death of vaudeville. If it hadn't been for the demise of this American form of popular entertainment, the stage of children's literature might never have been graced by the great comic presence of Sid Fleischman!

Albert Sidney Fleischman was born in Brooklyn, New York, in 1920. When he was two, his family relocated to San Diego, California, where he grew up and began an adolescent love affair with magic. Determined to become a professional magician, Fleischman read every book about magic he could find and, finally exhausting the supply of the San Diego Public Library, wrote one of his own, a book of original magic tricks that was published when he was nineteen.

Barely out of his teens, he then toured with a magic show

"during the last twenty minutes of vaudeville."[1] The tour took him through the American Midwest and the Great Plains states, where his California ear was surprised and delighted at hearing a "different English," which employed "roll-your-own imagery."

Intrigued by these new sounds, Fleischman found their well-springs in frontier diaries. He developed a passion for reading them—"the more illiterate the better"—finding, as he put it years later, that "words are kind of magical things, too." And not only the words that, strung together, comprised the folk speech of the nineteenth-century American frontier, but the names on the land and on those who settled it. Fleischman recalls his first encounter with one of those names. "I stepped into an elevator and saw a sign there for a 'Dr. Rattlefinger.'"

It stuck in his memory and was the first name he recorded in a book of names that he has kept ever since and that provides the names for most of the characters in his books. He recalls another example from some years later: He was taking his family for a Sunday drive in California's San Fernando Valley when he saw a sign advertising the Praisewater Mortuary. By the time he had gotten home to record the name in his book, he "misremembered" it and wrote down "Praiseworthy" instead. It was a happy accident, since—some years later—it provided the perfect name for the butler in his second children's book, *By the Great Horn Spoon!* (1963).

With the ultimate death of vaudeville, Fleischman began his college education, which was interrupted by service in World War II. Completing college after the end of the war, he found employment as a journalist for a San Diego newspaper. In due (or perhaps undue) course, the newspaper—like vaudeville before it—died. Instead of looking for other employment as a journalist,

Fleischman sat down instead and wrote a novel for adults (*The Straw Donkey Case*), which was published with a "fair degree of success for those times."

Eleven other books for adults followed (ten novels and one more book about magic). By this time Fleischman had three small children who hadn't the faintest idea what their father did for a living except that, as Fleischman recalls, "I stayed home all day and typed a lot."

To demonstrate that he was a novelist, he undertook the writing of a book specifically for them, reading each chapter aloud to the children as it was completed, a habit he would continue with subsequent books. Inevitably he found he had written a complete book and sent it off, a bit apologetically, to his agent, noting "I seem to have written a children's book. Throw it in the wastebasket if you're not interested." The agent *was* interested, of course, and so was Little, Brown, which published *Mr. Mysterious and Company* in 1962 and, hey, presto! a new career as a children's book author was launched.

"Life is full of happy surprises," Fleischman says.

It is, perhaps, no surprise at all—considering the conditions of its composition—that *Mr. Mysterious* should have as its protagonist a magician who has three children. Nor that the setting should be the American frontier of the nineteenth century—Texas, 1884, to be more specific.

When the reader first encounters them, Mr. Mysterious and his family are en route via covered wagon to a new home in California. Along the way they earn their keep by presenting magic shows in the small frontier towns through which they pass. Accordingly Pa has dubbed the covered wagon "our traveling temple of mystification, education, and jollification" (p. 43).

These three words are perfect shorthand descriptions of this book and the many others that would follow. Fleischman's plots, for example, are full of mystifications, odd twists, and surprising turnings (sometimes even surprising their author, who doesn't plot in advance and admits that he has to sit down at the typewriter [or, more recently, word processor] to discover what is going to happen next to his characters). Though the author considers his plots secondary to his characters, he does believe that his early experience of creating magic tricks helps with the working out of the plots.

As for education, his period novels are the result of prodigious research to guarantee the authenticity of their detail. Fleischman keeps a research book for each novel he writes and recalls that in doing background for his third book, *By the Great Horn Spoon!*, the story of a Boston boy's journey to the California gold fields and his experiences there, he read "forty or fifty" books about the period, including "all of Bancroft" (Hubert Howe Bancroft, 1832–1918, the American historian whose 60,000-volume personal library formed the nucleus of the University of California's Bancroft Library in Berkeley). Part of Fleischman's genius as a period novelist is his capacity to introduce such historical accuracies so seamlessly into his narratives that the reader is unaware of the extraordinary amount of historical "education" he is receiving as he reads. In *Mr. Mysterious*, for example, the reader learns about magic lantern shows, barter, traveling wagon shows, and more. In *Great Horn Spoon!* we learn about sea voyages around Cape Horn, life in the California gold fields, and such odd nuggets of historical fact as that forty-niners shipped their shirts all the way to China to be laundered! Fleischman himself seems to be bemused by such whimsical historical incidentals: "I had always regarded history as dignified as all get-out, but with this incident

I discovered that the past assays out fairly rich in comic ore."[2]

As for "jollification"? Well, John Rowe Townsend says, "Fleischman is in fact a humorist and the modern master of the tall tale."[3] Jane Yolen agrees: "He has made the particular voice of the tall tale so much his own that, if any one author can be said to be master of the genre, it is he."[4]

The evidence is everywhere in his books, lying about like nuggets on a gold field. Consider *By the Great Horn Spoon!* Like his other period novels, it is carefully rooted in historical reality: "It was not once upon a time," he notes on the very first page, "it was precisely the twenty-seventh day of January in the year 1849. Gold had been discovered in California some twelve months before and now, in a rush, the Gold Rush was on."

Rushing to California are two stowaways aboard the good ship *Lady Wilma*: young Jack Flagg, a Boston schoolboy of twelve, and his companion, "an elegant gentleman in a black broadcloth coat" (p. 4). The latter is, of course, the unflappable gentleman's gentleman (or in this case, Jack's gentleman) Praiseworthy, the butler.

The two are headed for the gold fields to strike it rich and restore the fading Flagg family fortunes. With the premise established, the fun gets under way: Much of it, at first, derives from the incongruity of the elegant Praiseworthy's presence amidst the rough and tumble of shipboard life.

"What in tarnation *are* you in that getup?" Captain Swan, "the wild bull of the seas," bellows.

"'I am a butler, sir.'

"'A butler!' the captain roared. 'A butler! What in the name of Old Scratch can a *butler* do?'

"'It's the other way around, sir,' said Praiseworthy, who took pride in his calling. 'There's nothing a butler *cannot* do'" (p. 14).

The angrier the apoplectic captain becomes, the more imperturbably unflappable Praiseworthy remains. The contrast is wildly funny. And funnier still when Praiseworthy later encounters an even wilder rage, the weather off Cape Horn:

"The *Lady Wilma* went teetering over on her side. . . . Jack, who had just sat down to a bowl of chowder, saw the bowl fly off in one direction, the chowder in another, and the spoon in a third.

"'I do believe we've arrived off the Horn,' said Praiseworthy, hanging onto his bowler hat" (p. 53).

Moments later seawater comes rushing along the deck and slipping down the hatches "like so many waterfalls" (p. 53), and Praiseworthy, now "holding onto a post with the hook of his black umbrella," calmly dismisses the raging weather as "a mere squall," adding, "Why, in these latitudes this is considered a fine spring day, I believe" (p. 53). Such admirable—no, *praiseworthy*—understatement puts even that of Doctor Dolittle in the shade.

As delightfully funny as the voyage is, the book doesn't hit its full comic stride until it reaches the California gold fields where, as Constance Rourke has observed, "With all the vicissitudes, the heartbreak, the losses, the abundance of human failure, the comic mood arose irresistibly."[5]

This "comic mood" manifests itself in a variety of ways; one, certainly, being colorful and unusual names: Where else can you visit places called "Bedbug," "Whiskey Flat," or "Hangtown"? Or what about "Rough and Ready," "You Bet," and "Humbug"? Or where else can you meet up with the likes of "Buffalo John," "Jimmie-from-Town," "Pitch-Pine Billy Pierce," or "Mississippi MacFinn"? For, as Pitch-Pine himself observes, "A man ain't really accepted around here until he's won himself a nickname" (p. 118). It's a measure of Jack and Praiseworthy's acceptance that they quickly become "Jamoka Jack" and "Bullwhip," respectively.

Praiseworthy's nickname is evidence of the miners' own love of tall tales and hyperbole. His "nom de gold field" is rooted in fact: He actually does, in a rare show of passion, knock a robber unconscious with a devastating left hook (made even more devastating by his left glove's being packed with gold dust).

"Why look at that," an observer says "in awe": "Knocked that big fella fifteen feet *up hill!*" (p. 106).

The story spreads like the proverbial wildfire, becoming more exaggerated with each telling: "Knocked that outlaw seventeen feet. *Up* hill." (p. 128).

"Nineteen feet—the way it was told to me" (p. 128).

"Nineteen feet and *eleven* inches. They measured it" (p. 128).

Finally a whiskered miner shifts the lump of chewing tobacco in his mouth and says, "Stranger, you must have a fightin' arm like the butt end of a bullwhip. Pleased to have you in our town" (p. 128).

Funny names and extravagant exaggeration are joined by comic exclamations: "By grabs, here's a lad with stuffings!" (p. 15), "Merciful powers!" and, my personal favorite:

Praiseworthy, finally weary of trying to disabuse the miners of their exaggerated ideas of his prowess with fisticuffs, decides "If they preferred a tall tale to the facts, let them have it" (p. 129).

And so, when a miner persists, "Bullwhip, you was there. Exactly how far *was it?*" Bullwhip—uh, *Praiseworthy*—replies, "Gents, from where I was standing—it looked twenty-three feet at least!"

To which a miner, swallowing his cud of tobacco, exclaims, "O be joyful!" (p. 129).

Obviously the temptation is almost irresistible, when writing about Fleischman's work, to keep quoting it endlessly. There are, for instance, even more wonderful examples of inventive and elaborate frontier talk that beg to be shared: A stagecoach driver arriving in Hangtown observes: "Looks mighty quiet today. Don't see nobody standin' under a pine limb with his boots off the ground" (p. 110). Then there's the justice of the peace who tells Praiseworthy, "Speakin' for myself, I don't see any reason to let law interfere with justice around here. We never did before" (p. 166).

And, of course, there's endless comic simile and metaphor: "My stomach feels like a cat in Hades without claws" (p. 137), "as heavy as a plummet" (p. 144), or "he don't know B from a bull's foot to make a statement like that" (p. 141).

Wonderfully funny and comic as all of these humorous devices are, they are only so many flecks of gold dust compared to the true mother lode of humor that enriches the book. Constance Rourke has identified this in her observation: "In a sense the whole American comic tradition had been that of social criticism."[6]

For American readers the most permanent pleasure of the book derives from watching Praiseworthy reinvent himself on the untamed frontier, transforming himself from a butler, born to his "calling" of gentleman's gentleman, into his own (gentle)man. "Perhaps," he says, "it's time I shed the past myself. Out here," he finally realizes, "one man is as good as another."

"Only more so," adds Jack (p. 190), whose own . . . *praiseworthy* egalitarian feelings have finally found fruition in the butler's transformation into free man and—finally rid of his tightly rolled black umbrella and black bowler hat—free spirit.

In a later book, *Jingo Django* (1971), Fleischman will once again employ humor as social criticism when he offers a sympathetic portrait of a band of Gypsies and a scathing satirical portrait of those "good Americans" who have abused them. The Gypsies, too, are free spirits, but the freest spirit of all will be Uncle Will Buckthorn, the titular grand rascal of what is arguably Fleischman's finest book, *Chancy and the Grand Rascal* (1966).

In form it combines the tall tale with another, similar genre, the picaresque, a form that invites the creation of roguish protagonists and tongue-in-cheek accounts of their antic adventures. Fleischman confesses to a particular fondness for grand rascals, attributing it to his "magician's background" and explaining that such characters are not villains but have "magician-like minds," solving their problems by employing "sleight-of-mind" instead of "sleight-of-hand."

In form, tone, and character, *Chancy* is reminiscent of Robert Lewis Taylor's Pulitzer Prize–winning novel, *The Travels of Jamie McPheeters*, or his later novel *Journey to Matecumbe*.

Like these novels and Fleischman's own earlier *Great Horn Spoon!*, *Chancy* hangs its narrative on a quest, though this time not for gold-field riches but for young Chancy's scattered family: "It was four years ago that he had last seen his brother and sisters. After the death of their mother, the youngsters had been separated, scattered about the countryside like leaves on the wind" (p. 5).

Chancy is older and more self-reliant than Jack but not worldly enough when he first sets off on his own to see through the flimflammery of a frontier confidence man, the self-styled "Colonel" Plugg, who would obviously agree with the advice of that "crafty rascal" Simon Suggs: "It is good to be shifty in a new country."[7] (Suggs, the creation of Alabama humorist Johnson J. Hooper, first appeared in book form in 1845.)

By the time they part company, the shifty Colonel has possession of Chancy's steamboat fare, and all Chancy has are five dozen of the Colonel's "Ohio Wonder Eggs" ("Triple yolkers, you know" [p. 20]).

Once burned, twice shy. Even though the Colonel has turned out to be a sharpie, Chancy can't help remembering the rogue's advice: "never trust a man in a slouch hat. . . . A bad lot I'll tell you . . ." (p. 15) when he subsequently does meet up with a broad-shouldered man in . . . a dark slouch hat.

To his surprise, the man turns out to be none other than "the grand rascal in the family," his "wanderin', fiddle-footed uncle, Will Buckthorn" (p. 35).

To the reader's delight, Uncle Will is clearly cut from the same cloth as Davy Crockett and Mike Fink. Here's how he introduces himself to his stunned nephew: "Why, Chancy, I'm a coming-and-going man, that's who I am! I can shoe a runaway horse and out-calculate a pack of foxes. I'm half-fox myself, and the other half prairie buffalo." The reader will forgive him if he forgets to mention "ring-tailed roarer," since he quickly enough proves the truth of the rest of his brag: "I can out-laugh, out-exaggerate, and out-rascal any man this side of the Big Muddy" (p. 35).

Like *By the Great Horn Spoon!, Chancy and the Grand Rascal* is an exercise in tall-tale frontier humor. But the frontier here is not the gold fields of California but the rivers of middle America, the Ohio and the Mississippi. And the frontier types we encounter are not miners but river men—*big* men with "arms like swamp oaks" (p. 62). Men who match brag for brag, boast for boast, and lie for lie.

"I'm Captain Joe Harpe," one of them roars, "the bulliest raft pilot in sight. And the hog-hungriest" (p. 60). "To the oars, my lazy mud turtles," Harpe orders his crew, "step lively, you snoring, roaring river-rollers" (p. 66).

Ultimately, of course, Uncle Will wins over the captain and

turns him into an ally with a combination of sleight-of-mind, a sense of theater, and a tall-tale exhibition of strength.

To the captain's boast that "Any one of my boys is strong enough to derail a train—just squintin' at it," Uncle Will offers an incendiary reply: "They look kind of weak and sickly to me."

Stung to the core, the captain orders one of his crew, Billy Arkansas, to lift a prodigiously large boulder. "Shucks," Billy says, lifting it over his head, "this little ol' rock don't amount to a thing, Cap. Couldn't weigh more'n two hundred and fifty pounds" (p. 63).

Uncle Will's reply is to calmly lift Billy Arkansas, boulder and all, up onto his shoulders.

"'Glory be,' said Captain Harpe, his little eyes snapping in awe." And then, gracious in defeat, he urges, "Stranger, put down that weak and sickly raftsman of mine. Hoolah-haw! Welcome aboard, sir. You and the boy . . . stay as long as you like" (p. 65).

Chancy and Uncle Will ultimately leave the captain and the Mississippi River for a journey up the Missouri to Kansas City, but not before Uncle Will and the captain engage in an epic ("Hoolah-haw! Boys, give me lung room" [p. 146]) liars' contest. (Fleischman's research into the kind of gollywhoppers that were swapped in contests of this sort later inspired the creation of Josh McBroom and a whole series of books in which McBroom tells the delighted reader whoppers about his wonderful one-acre farm in Iowa.)

Meanwhile, in observing Uncle Will in action, we have already learned a great deal about the conventions of frontier lying and the art of swapping "stretchers": While gain for one party or the other might result, the act itself is a duel of wits and, no matter how outlandish the claims being made on credulity, the contest is conducted with a straight face ("Chancy never saw two more sober faces. It was as if the merest glimmer of a smile would break the rules and ruin the contest . . ." [p. 98]). As was the case with the tall tales about Paul Bunyan, the truth of the story is avowed even if it means disavowing an earlier version: Uncle Will says, "But I may have been departin' slightly from the facts, I'll admit that. The bona-fide, rock-bottomed, guaranteed facts are so hard to believe that you'd think I was trying to string up a bunch of nonsense" (p. 98). He then, of course, proceeds to offer an even more outrageous story.

John Rowe Townsend has compared Fleischman to the British writer Leon Garfield. And it is inarguably true that these two great writers share many areas of creativity—they both write period novels, they both love exaggerated, larger-than-life characters, they both are keenly witty observers of life and its injustices and absurdities, but more than anything else, they are both absolute, undisputed champion creators of dazzling similes and metaphors. Nowhere is this more evident than in *Chancy and the Grand Rascal*. Here are just a few: Chancy is so thin "he could take a bath in a shotgun barrel" (p. 34). His sister Indiana is "so thin [she] could fall through a stovepipe without getting sooty" (p. 126). His other sister, Mirandy, is "as contrary as a mule in a mud puddle" (p. 164).

Uncle Will is "straight-faced as a deacon" (p. 97).

A villain is "mean as his hide will hold" (p. 106). "That man's the devil, red-hot from home" (p. 119), and the prospect of money will bring him along "as sure as a goose goes barefoot" (p. 117).

And now, "quicker'n a frog can clear his throat" (p. 38), here are two others: "tighter than a new boot" (p. 42) and "about as easy to sell as toothpicks to a catfish" (p. 44).

Finally, "steady as a clock" (p. 4) reminds us that Uncle Will's profession (you can't put food on the table by telling lies) is that of clock salesman, although in the whole book we see him sell only one clock and that transaction inevitably involves a tall tale. To stop a cowboy from drowning a sackful of newborn kittens, Uncle Will convinces him that you can tell time by looking at a cat's eyes. ("It's all in the darks of the eyes—the way they widen and shrink with the daylight" [p. 157].) If you think the cowboy will get away with only one cat to tell the time by, you forget that Uncle Will is a *grand* rascal. And so, of course, he convinces the cowboy to take the whole litter: "I've known cats to run slow and run fast. After you get the hang of it, you'll know which one makes the best timepiece" (p. 158). Of course, while the cowboy is learning to tell cat time, he'll need a regular clock, and Uncle Will just "happens" to have one left.

By the time the cowboy goes on his way, he has a sack of kittens and a clock.

And Uncle Will has an additional ten dollars.

And everybody's happy—even Fleischman, who admits this is his favorite story in the book, and one that was actually current on the Western frontier.

Aside from their inspired play with the English language, both Garfield and Fleischman are masters of establishing richly realized and historically accurate settings. Garfield's landscape is, of course, English, and his signature century is the seventeenth. Fleischman, as we have already demonstrated, sets his stories on the emerging Middle Western and Western frontier in *his* signature century, the nineteenth.

In addition to being compared to each other, Garfield and Fleischman also have in common inevitable comparisons with, respectively, Charles Dickens and Mark Twain. It is outside the scope of this book to explore Dickens's influence on Garfield, but the point might be made that a Dickensian influence shows up in Fleischman's work as well—especially in the richness of his settings, his humorous view of life, the wittiness of his language, the extravagance and eccentricity of his characters (notably his villains), and his social conscience. This last consideration is particularly apparent in *Jingo Django*, in which, as we have discussed earlier, the author presents a sympathetic and insightful portrait of a band of Gypsies and also creates a positively Dickensian orphanage (Mrs. Daggatt's Beneficent Orphan House), which Oliver Twist would recognize in a twinkling.

As for the Twain influence, the spirit of Mark Twain, the young City Editor of the *Virginia City Enterprise* and author of *Roughing It*, certainly informs Fleischman's *Boston Globe–Horn Book* Award–winning *Humbug Mountain* (1978). In it we meet Wiley, his sister, Glorietta, and their father, the itinerant newspaper publisher "Colonel" Rufus Flint. The Colonel finds opportunity in the fact that "As frontier settlements expanded into thriving communities, an essential commodity was the local newspaper."[8] Frequently insolvent (like Twain) and plagued by a bad case of the "yonders" (again like Twain, who boasted, "I believe I have not spent six months in one place . . . since 1853"[9]) Wiley and Glorietta's Pa moves from town to town. Of course, this is sometimes not due to his own wanderlust but because, as Wiley notes, "more than once we were run out of town. . . . I've seen men come looking for him with a horsewhip or worse just because Pa had said in print they were lop-eared donkeys or corn-cribbing crooks. Newspapermen are given to strong language like that" (pp. 4–5). Indeed, Twain once called a Nevada politician "a long-legged, bull-headed, whopper-jawed, constructionary monomaniac."[10]

With no prospects, the Colonel decides to take his family to his father-in-law's newly founded town of Sunrise, "The Parnassus of the West," somewhere up the Missouri, at the foot of Humbug Mountain.

And a humbug it is. Arriving there, the family discovers, to its shock, that "There was no town. Sunrise was just a scrap of paper" (p. 38). Similarly, Grandpa is nowhere to be found, but there, smack-dab in the middle of the dry-as-a-bone desolation, in the very center of an empty creek bottom, sits Grandpa's riverboat, *The Phoenix*.

The incongruity of a riverboat's sitting high and dry in the dusty middle of nowhere epitomizes the tone of this book, which is rich in hoax and humbug. Twain would recognize one hoax immediately: Wiley, poking about in the dirt, discovers the body of a petrified man, which will later turn out to be "a dad-blasted fake!" Twain himself contrived a similar fake, reporting at length in the *Enterprise* about the discovery of a petrified man who had been dead for ten generations.

Later, to rid *The Phoenix* and his family of two wanted-by-the-law desperadoes, the Colonel agrees to publish a fake account of their deaths in a newspaper, which he will create for that purpose: *The Humbug Mountain Hoorah*. ("Yes," the Colonel muses, "*humbug* strikes just the right note" [p. 63]).

The best hoax, however, is not revealed until the end of the book, and it is one that not only evokes the spirit of Mark Twain but also links *Humbug Mountain* securely to the tall-tale tradition. Early in the book we have learned that Wiley's personal passion is for reading "nickel novel" accounts of the heroic exploits of that larger-than-life frontier hero Quickshot Billy Bodeen, "King of the Tin Stars."

As the book nears its climax, who should show up, riding shotgun for Grampa on his new boat, but—well, let Wiley tell it:

"There he stood. Quickshot Billy Bodeen in person. He wore a big white Stetson hat, just like he wore in the book pictures, but his legs were so bowed you could run a hog through them. And you could hardly see his gunbelt for his stomach hanging over it. He looked as blown up as a colicky horse. I wondered how he located his guns for his famous quick draw" (p. 139).

Based on this description, I suppose that one could say that Quickshot in the flesh was as much larger than life as his reputation—but in all the wrong places.

The nickel novel accounts of Billy's exploits, thus, have about as much validity as the comic-book stories Homer Price and his friend Freddy read about "Super-Duper."

Hyperbole is great humorous fun, but for heroism, Fleischman and McCloskey suggest, we must look to ourselves and to our wits. In the final analysis, super strength is no substitute for sleight-of-mind.

Fleischman's own use of hyperbole reaches its apogee in the McBroom books, which are notable for their stupefyingly inventive lies about the productivity of McBroom's wonderful one-acre farm. Highly anecdotal in form, they are delightfully witty but are best taken in small doses, rather like the authentic oral versions of tall-tale hero stories. Their form dictates that they will be sketchy in their narrative content and will lack fully developed characters with whom the reader can become involved. McBroom's first-person narrative voice is delightfully droll, however, and consistently amusing in its deadpan retailing of colossal whoppers as the gospel truth.

The truth about Sid Fleischman is, simply, that he has one of the most consistently accomplished humorous voices in American literature for children. I can think of no other writer who so brilliantly demonstrates the comic possibilities of the language itself and the glorious fun that can be had with it. The Newbery Medal he won for *The Whipping Boy* (1986) (ironically, a book *not* set in America) was a long-overdue recognition of his status at the forefront of American children's literature.

"Comedy is easily misread as the mere vaudeville of literature," this former vaudevillian has written.[11] Unfortunately too many critics have agreed and have, accordingly, relegated humor to the wings of the stage.

It is Sid Fleischman's great contribution to children and their literature to have brought humor out from the wings to center stage, where it deserves and, indeed, *needs* to be.

Notes

[1] Except as otherwise indicated, all the direct quotations in this chapter are taken from my February 1987 interview with Sid Fleischman for the television program *In Print*.

[2] Fleischman, Sid, "Laughter and Children's Literature," *The Horn Book*, LII: 468 (October 1976).

[3] Townsend, John Rowe, *Written for Children* (3rd rev. ed.). New York: J. B. Lippincott, 1987, p. 209.

[4] Yolen, Jane, "Fleischman, (Albert) Sid(ney)," in *Twentieth-Century Children's Writers* (3rd ed.), edited by Tracy Chevalier. Chicago: St. James Press, 1989, p. 351.

[5] Rourke, Constance, *American Humor: A Study of the National Character*. New York: Harcourt, Brace and Co., 1931, p. 209.

[6] Rourke, p. 211.

[7] Blair, Walter, *Native American Humor (1800–1900)*. New York: American Book Co., 1937, p. 86.

[8] Inge, M. Thomas, *The Frontier Humorists*. Hamden, Conn.: Archon Books, 1975, p. 2.

[9] Quoted in Lauber, John, *The Making of Mark Twain*. New York: American Heritage, 1985, p. 104.

[10] Quoted in Lauber, p. 112.

[11] Fleischman, p. 466.

Chapter Seven

....

HUMOR AT HOME

....

"Happy families are all alike;
every unhappy family is unhappy in its own way."
—*Tolstoy,* Anna Karenina

"Because, Mom, everybody's family is not like ours."
—*Betsy Byars,* The Blossoms and the Green Phantom

"It's just jolly . . . it's just jolly to get home."
—*Margaret Sidney,* Five Little Peppers and How They Grew

Since the publication of Louisa May Alcott's classic novel *Little Women* in 1868, the celebration of family life and its setting, the home, has been a staple of American children's literature and one of its significant contributions to the larger world of books for young readers. In fact, British critic Marcus Crouch points to Alcott's very American book as a progenitor of the English family story and concludes that "one of the healthiest strains in the story of family life has come out of America."[1]

Ironically this "healthy" strain sprang out of a historic moment—the immediate post–Civil War period—when insecurity powerfully visited the lives of young readers residing in a singularly unhealthy nation, one that had been nearly destroyed by the assassination of its president, by the rigors of Reconstruction, and by the sundering effects of the Civil War, which had ended only two years before the publication of the landmark *Little Women*.

The war had robbed many families of fathers—at least temporarily—and even those the war had spared may well have been missing a father who had gone ahead to establish a new place for them on a still-expanding frontier. The March sisters' father is himself absent, serving as a chaplain in the Civil War, duty from which he may or may not return. Left to bear the full responsibility for the feeding, comfort, and well-being of the family, mothers like Mrs. March were as burdened as those whose absent husbands were carving out a new frontier. In a recent biography of Daniel Boone, John Mack Faragher makes a similar point: "It was the labor of women, in fact, that made possible men's hunting. With men so frequently away from the homestead, many women became the sole support for their families." When he concludes by saluting "the strength and determination of an able and intelligent woman [Rebecca Boone], the center of an affectionate and close family,"[2] he salutes not only historically real women but fictional ones, like Mrs. March and, later, Mrs. Pepper and Mrs. Moffat.

The theme of the protagonist's search for father and family, which informs so many of Sid Fleischman's historical novels, is, as we can see in this context, an accurate reflection of the social reality of much of the nineteenth century—it is surely significant that the two liveliest boy characters of American nineteenth-century literature, Tom Sawyer and Huckleberry Finn, are essentially parentless—Tom being an orphan and Huck a ward of the Widow Douglas.

Tom Sawyer and *Huckleberry Finn* aside—neither being, by any stretch of the imagination, exemplars of the "domestic" novel—the nineteenth-century family story is typically one of hard-won survival, the struggle to overcome the long odds of family disruption and economic privation. No wonder humor is not one of its hallmarks; critic Jerry Griswold calls *Little Women* "this remorseful book" and reminds us that Alcott at one time intended the book's title to be *The Pathetic Family.*[3]

What is arguably the second-most-popular family story of the nineteenth century—Margaret Sidney's *Five Little Peppers and How They Grew*—continues this theme, in spades. First published in book form in 1881 (individual stories about the Peppers having earlier appeared in the magazine *Wide Awake*), the novel sold more than a million copies in its first fifty years in print. (It's intriguing that the pseudonymous Mrs. Sidney—whose real name was Harriet Lothrop; she was the wife of the book's publisher, Daniel Lothrop—lived for a time at "The Wayside," the house in Concord, Massachusetts, that had been the erstwhile home of the Alcott family and the setting for *Little Women.*)

The Pepper children, like the Marches, suffer from an absent father, though there is no question about the possibility of *his* return: "The father had died when Phronsie was a baby."

Accordingly, "Mrs. Pepper had had hard work to scrape together money enough to put bread into her children's mouths and to pay the rent of the Little Brown House.

"But she had met life too bravely to be beaten down now. So, with a stout heart and a cheery face, she had worked away day after day at making coats, and tailoring and mending of all descriptions" (p. 1).

The five *little* Peppers are as relentlessly cheery as their mother as they bustle about attempting to realize their "great ambition," which is, of course, "'To help mother'" (p. 2). The Peppers are, in fact, so perpetually positive, so unfailingly upbeat, that the modern reader wants to tell them to cheer *down*, for God's sake!

This same relentless spirit of good cheer informs the three Moffat books by Eleanor Estes, whose work—though published sixty years later—seems certainly to have been inspired by the Peppers' example. (Estes grew up in West Haven, Connecticut, a residential suburb of New Haven, where Lothrop spent *her* early years.)

Consider that the Moffat children (there are four of them: Sylvie, Joey, Jane, and Rufus) are fatherless, Papa having died when Rufus was just "a tiny baby." "Times are bad" for the Moffats (*The Moffats*, 1941, p. 15), who live (ironically) on New Dollar Street, and Mama, "the best dressmaker in the village of Cranbury" (p. 19), "was having to be a very careful manager to make ends meet" (p. 172).

"'Are we poverty-stricken, Mama?'" Jane asked. . . .

"'No, Janey. Not poverty-stricken,' said Mama soberly . . . 'just poor'" (p. 172). (It's a delightful, though probably incidental, irony that a Moffat family appears in *Little Women* too, but those Moffats are wealthy, the sumptuous circumstances of their lives tempting Meg March to envy, and to sigh, "to be rich" [p. 81].)

Like the Peppers, the Moffat children are enterprising and cheerfully determined to help their struggling mother. Similarly, the "Little Brown House" in which the Peppers live and the "yellow house" where the Moffats reside are hugely important in the families' respective lives. All Mrs. Pepper asks is that "we keep together . . . and grow up good, so that the Little Brown House won't be ashamed of us . . ." (p. 10). The threat that the yellow house will be sold (the Moffats rent it) is the theme that unifies the episodic chapters of the first book of their adventures, *The Moffats*. The "middle Moffat," nine-year-old Jane, anxiously contemplating this possibility, tells her doll Hildegarde, "'Maybe no one will have the money to buy the house. . . .' And suddenly all the warmth and familiarity of the yellow house came back to her with a rush" (p. 19).

While the Moffat books may owe much in the way of inspiration and example to the Peppers, they are vastly superior as works of fiction (though hardly unflawed). In terms of literary history the Moffat books may be seen as a bridge between the period family story (that of the nineteenth century) and the modern family story. Though published in 1941, 1942, and 1943, respectively, the three Moffat books (*The Moffats*, *The Middle Moffat*, and *Rufus M.*) are set at the time of World War I, and in their tone, as well as in the details of their setting, they are oddly old-fashioned.

Estes, who was born in 1906, recalls that West Haven was "a perfect town to grow up in,"[4] and she has lovingly re-created her hometown, as it was during her own growing-up years, in the fictional village of Cranbury, where the Moffats live and which, in a not insignificant sense, is as much a "home" (without walls) as the yellow house is. Because Cranbury provides security and sanctuary and because the reader quickly realizes nothing *really* bad will happen to the Moffats, an air of genial good humor suffuses all the stories (while at the same time compromising any element of suspense). Though sometimes unreadable because of their tone (discussed in detail below), the Moffat books are significant for introducing elements of humor into the family story and for prefiguring, thus, the more robust and genuinely funny domestic comedy of Beverly Cleary, Lois Lowry, and Betsy Byars.

Indeed, aside from their pervasive sense of well-being and family-generated security, it is probably their gentle humor that has made these stories, about small events that loom large in children's lives, so enduringly popular. At that, the humor is more likely to provoke a smile than a laugh. Consider some of the devices she employs.

First of all, she knows the humorous potential of funny names: Mama amuses her children by telling them about her cousin "Julius Hausenchausenpschutzler". But it's unlikely that modern readers will react as . . . *vigorously* to this drollery as "Rufus [who] . . . could never hear that name without nearly splitting himself in the middle with laughter" (*Moffats*, p. 166).

There is also the occasional mildly funny exclamation, Rufus's personal favorite being "Crimanenty!" (For his part Joel Pepper likes to say "My whockety!" to which his sister—shades of Walter R. Brooks's Aunt Effie—chides, "Don't say such dreadful words, Joel . . . 'tisn't nice" [p. 5].)

There is some mild satire, too, usually involving "progress" (à la *Homer Price*). For example, "the whole town" agrees that it is "a fine thing, very modern to have [a] new trolley line" (p. 231). Inevitably, however, this modern wonder leads to confusion and contretemps and to at least one outraged citizen's contemptuous dismissal of "Newfangled notions, these one-man trolleys with their one-track contraptions!" (*Moffats*, p. 238).

"Culture" is also satirized in the perhaps too-easy target of the ladies of the local Browning Society, who, inspired by the example of Thoreau, decide to simplify their individual and collective lives by giving certain of their material possessions away. The Moffats are not too proud to accept many of these castoffs (if Cranbury is an extension of their home, then everyone who lives there is a member of an extended Moffat family), but the real humor comes in the nonsensical strategy that one of the ladies, Mrs. Price, employs to choose the thing she will give away: She closes her eyes, turns around three times, and points. Unfortunately what she points at (her parlor organ) is something she *doesn't* want to give away. And so she repeats the procedure. Predictably she points at the organ a second time, and so, getting dizzier, she turns around a third time and, inevitably, points at—well, the upshot is that the Moffats wind up the proud owners of a new parlor organ.

Later in this same story ("The Organ Recital," from *The Middle Moffat*), the Browning Society ladies will provide a moment of slapstick humor when they are routed from the Moffats' parlor by an eruption of moths from the organ's innards during Jane's—uh—*spirited* recital. ("'Oh, oh, oh! Run, girls, run!' screamed one of the ladies and they all made for the door, with moths settling on their hair-nets and even getting down their necks" [p. 48].)

The most enduring humor of the three books, however, derives not from incident or attitude or language, but from the character of Jane, the only one of the four children to be a completely (and engagingly) developed character.

Perhaps the only child character outside Dickens to actually suffer from chilblains, Jane—like Arnold Lobel's Toad—is a worrywart: She imagines that if the family is, indeed, poverty-stricken, "she would have to go out into the cold and into the streets and sell matches like the little match girl" (*Moffats*, p. 172). On another occasion, having been unable to resist making fun of the pompous and self-important Mr. Pennypepper, the new Superintendent of Schools (who does, indeed, *love* to give speeches!), Jane then indulges herself in agonies of worry that she will be arrested for her irreverence.

Still later in the series, she will be overcome by guilt that none of the Moffats has joined the new church gymnasium (despite the minister's sermonizing that "the gymnasium belongs to you. To all of you" [*Middle*, p. 207]). And so "Janey Takes Up Sports," finding in herself a surprising facility for basketball, since she is normally the kind of athlete who throws a croquet ball up in the air and then, losing it in the sun, "catches" it with her head. ("It had staggered her but she had walked off in silent dignity . . ." [p. 210].)

As this demonstrates, one thing that makes Jane such an engaging and amusing character is the fact that young readers can simultaneously empathize with her and feel superior to her. Another—to adult readers, at least—is the obvious fact that Jane is the character with whom the author herself has the closest rapport; in fact, Estes, in her own real life, would have been almost exactly Jane's age at the time in which the Moffat books are set.

What also sets Jane apart from her more practical siblings is that she is a dreamer who likes to look at the world from a fresh perspective: upside down. ("It was wonderful to look at things from between her legs, upside down. Everything had a different look altogether, a much cleaner, brighter look" [*Moffats*, pp. 9–10].) And despite her fears and worries, she enjoys doing unusual things ("Their sister Jane sometimes did extremely curious things, [her siblings] agreed" [*Moffats*, p. 196]), including walking under horses and assuming personal responsibility for ensuring that Cranbury's "Oldest Inhabitant" survives to his one hundredth birthday. One can easily imagine that Jane, with such an offbeat imagination, could grow up to be a writer—like Eleanor Estes, perhaps. . . .

Unfortunately, Estes does not bring the same invention and empathy to the other Moffat children—indeed, one feels that the two older children, Sylvie and Joe, are largely window dressing.

And as a fictional character, the youngest child, Rufus, is at best a bit of an embarrassment. For unlike the very real Jane, he is not a real character at all but only an adult's idealized and sentimentalized vision of what a "real" boy would be like. The result is a too-perky infant who suffers from an advanced case of what I might call "Shirley Temple Syndrome"; that is, he is insufferably precious, cute, cunning, and arch. "Even God has to go to school," he tendentiously informs his neighbor, Hughie, a reluctant student.

In another story he forgets himself and laughs out loud at the public library with the following unfortunate result: "Rufus clapped his chubby fist over his mouth. Goodness! He had forgotten where he was. Do not laugh or talk out loud in the library. He knew these rules . . ." (*Rufus M.*, p. 9).

Unfortunately Estes forgets the rules of good character creation and development when she writes about the youngest Moffat. She cannot seem to represent his point of view without interjecting a tone of adult editorializing and condescension. Consider the following examples: "He liked the pictures, but goodness! would he ever be able to read those words?" (*Moffats*, p. 55). "Goodness, this train was just speeding along" (*Moffats*, p. 69). "It looked familiar to him and he hoped it was his. It was! Hurrah!" (*Rufus M.*, p. 43–44).

Rufus is also too often the inspiration for what *The New Yorker* magazine might dub "Chuckles we doubt ever got chuckled!" Examples: "But of course he wouldn't have much time for watching trains, he chuckled, if he ever wanted to catch up with [his older brother Joey] in school" (*Moffats*, p. 55). And—my favorite—"Goodness," he chuckled, "if Santy brought a pony for every letter I wrote! . . . But I guess he'll know better than that" (*Middle*, p. 148).

Estes should know better than that too, for the tone of this treatment is so inherently patronizing that the reader has to wonder whose point of view is being represented.

And even inviting such speculation by the reader is the quickest possible way for an author to destroy empathy with a character. At her most self-indulgent, Estes applies the same mistake of tone, voice, and conflicted point of view to her other characters—the tipoff that such a transgression is in the offing typically being a flurry of exclamation points: "What a nice man this was!" (Joey) (*Moffats*, p. 80). "That trolley ride! There was something to tell Mama about!" (Jane) (*Moffats*, p. 243). "How he hated to leave that nice, safe place by the piano!" (Joey again) (*Moffats*, p. 144). This device reaches a kind of breathless frenzy in the final chapter of *The Moffats* where, on page 244, there are four exclamation points in the space of five sentences.

If there is a lesson for would-be humorists in the Moffat books, it is their inadvertent demonstration of the ultimate irony of humor: that despite its roots in incongruity, all its constituent elements—tone, point of view, authorial attitude, etc.—must be congruent, or the humor fails.

It is not an easy lesson to learn, and in fact even Beverly Cleary, the author who is Estes's logical successor in the evolution of family humor, and the creator, in Ramona Quimby, of one of modern children's literature's greatest characters, makes some of the same mistakes, as we will discover in a moment. But first a few words of context from Maurice Sendak.

"The great theme for any child," Sendak reflected recently, "is how to survive the next twenty-four hours. This means defeating boredom, and handling the overwhelming questions of death and loss and getting mad, and then going upstairs and having supper."[5]

Real children are helped with managing these problems by reading books in which fictional counterparts deal humorously and successfully with similar problems. One of the most enduringly popular of these counterparts is Beverly Cleary's Ramona Quimby, who made her first appearance as a pesty neighborhood supernumerary in Cleary's 1950s Henry Huggins books. She quickly took over center stage, however, thanks to a personality so vivid that one critic has described her as "a force of nature."[6]

Most readers who have met Ramona will presume, more specifically, that the force of nature in question is a hurricane or an earthquake or, at the very least, a tidal wave sweeping across the narrative landscape and disrupting the order it finds there.

When we first encounter Ramona in a book that bears her name—never mind that she gets second billing in the title, *Beezus and Ramona* (1955); she is very much the star—she is four and here is what we see: "Ramona, holding a mouth organ in her teeth, was riding around the room on her tricycle. Since she needed both hands to steer the tricycle, she could blow in and out on only one note. This made the harmonica sound as if it were groaning *oh dear, oh dear* over and over again. Beezus tried to pay no attention" (p. 9).

This, of course, proves impossible, and even readers who have not previously met Ramona in the Henry Huggins books will quickly understand why the first line of this book is "Beatrice Quimby's biggest problem was her little sister Ramona" (p. 7).

Cleary has written about the genesis of the Ramona books as being her awakening understanding "that children would enjoy a book about a younger girl because they would recognize and enjoy feeling superior to their younger selves . . . humor is a way of relieving anxiety; children enjoy feeling superior to their younger selves and are relieved to know they've grown."[7]

This notion is reinforced in this first book by presenting the six stories it contains from Beezus's point of view. In later books, when Ramona's point of view has assumed control of the narrative, a younger neighbor girl, Willa Jean will provide "the younger self" to feel superior to. In turn, she will become as reliable a source of annoyance to Ramona as Ramona had been to Beezus: "People said Willa Jean behaved just the way Ramona used to, but Ramona could not believe them" (*Ramona and Her Father*, 1977, p. 154).

In addition to the superiority humor so important to *Beezus and Ramona*, Cleary employs other humorous devices as well.

As previously indicated, Ramona's introduction of disorder and barely controlled chaos into the Quimby household is one. Another is repetition and its corollary, anticipation. For example: Since it has been vividly established that disaster will ensue whenever Ramona gets on her tricycle, the reader will automatically smile in anticipation every time she does this. The anticipation and, thus, the humor are heightened further when an unusual point of view—that of Henry's dog, Ribsy—is briefly introduced:

"Ribsy lay on the rug near Henry and warily watched Ramona, who was wearing her rabbit ears and riding her tricycle around the living room" (*Beezus*, p. 65).

This invites the delighted reader to speculate about what new disaster Ramona is about to perpetrate—perhaps involving poor Ribsy (and, indeed, poor Ribsy *does* get involved!).

A similar situation involving Beezus is funny for the same reason: Left in charge, she decides that reading to Ramona about Big Steve, the steam shovel—something she normally despises doing—"would be the easiest way to keep Ramona from thinking up some mischief to get into while Mother was away" (p. 88).

"A Party at the Quimbys'," the story usually regarded as

the funniest in the book, incorporates all the above elements: Ramona, determined to have a "par-tee," invites a houseful of children to the Quimbys' without bothering to tell her mother. ("'Where do you suppose she found them all?' whispered Beezus. 'I don't even know some of them'" [p. 110].) To make matters worse, it's raining outside and Mrs. Quimby—not knowing a par-tee is in the offing—has just washed everybody's hair. While Mrs. Quimby and Beezus try to cope, the children decide to play parade and march about the house screaming "Bingle-bongle-by!" Each time relative calm returns, the parade deafeningly reappears ("Bingle-bongle-by!"), and the reader is reduced to helpless laughter imagining Mrs. Quimby and Beezus grinding their teeth in frustration.

Though more vividly written and featuring more realistic characters, *Beezus and Ramona* is squarely in the tradition of the Moffat books. Although Ramona has two parents, the father is essentially absent from this book. Episodic in construction, it celebrates small moments in the life of everychild: being read to from a favorite book, going to the library, riding a tricycle around the house, hectoring an older sibling, enjoying your imagination (and the pet lizard it conjures up!)—all the quiet (well, from Ramona's point of view) pleasures of the quotidian. The things that happen in this first Ramona book could have happened to any of the Moffats. Indeed, the first story in the book ("Beezus and Her Little Sister") recounts, in part, Ramona's determination to get her own library card, echoing precisely the premise of the first story in *Rufus M.*, wherein Rufus is equally determined to get *his* own card. (In fact, in this story at least, Rufus could give *Ramona* lessons in singlemindedness!)

In each story a child must be able to demonstrate that he or she can write his/her own name to get a card. Rufus thinks the librarian is talking about a playing card, while Ramona, going to the "charging desk," thinks at first that you have to *pay* for the books. The inferred or naïve pun (a child's too-literal misunderstanding of a word that has an implicit double meaning) is a reliable source of superiority humor in both the Moffat and Ramona books, as well as, later, in the Anastasia Krupnik books when Anastasia's little brother, Sam's, point of view is invoked. (More about this later.)

Finally, it should be noted that both kids bear down too hard with the writing instrument of their choice (Ramona breaks the point of her pencil and Rufus's knuckles turn white).

The real humor of this first Ramona book, however, is rooted in the recognizable conflict that arises between siblings and in the vividly realized character of Ramona herself, who is surely everychild and definitely everylittlesister. (Cleary has noted, regarding the children who write letters to her, "An amazing number have little brothers or sisters exactly like Ramona."[8])

In her unbridled candor, her imagination "a mile long" (p. 40), and her singlemindedness Ramona has a genius for embarrassing her older sister. Embarrassment is a universal affliction—teenagers choose to be embarrassed by their parents rather than their younger siblings—and reading about it provides relief, release, and the inevitable accompanying smile.

There are more smiles of this sort in what might be called the sequel to Beezus and Ramona—*Ramona the Pest* (1968). As the title suggests, Ramona is the undisputed star of this book, a fact that is demonstrated by all the stories' being told from her unqualified point of view. Ramona is now five and is entering kindergarten. Like Rufus, Ramona has looked forward to going to school: "She had been waiting years just to get to kindergarten" (p. 14). Rufus thinks, of *his* first day in school, "Why, he had looked forward to this day for years, it seemed to him" (*Moffats*, p. 51).

By taking Ramona out of her house in this book, Cleary expands her world and begins to include adults as viable characters, a feature that will grow increasingly important in subsequent books such as *Ramona and Her Father* and *Ramona and Her Mother* (1979).

Being removed from her family during the school day will also cause Ramona to suffer her first identity crisis: In the chapter titled "The Baddest Witch in the World," she dresses as a witch for the school's Halloween party. At first she is pleased that no one recognizes her, but very quickly she is overwhelmed by this enforced anonymity: "The feeling was the scariest one Ramona had ever experienced . . . the thought that her own mother might not know her frightened Ramona even more."

In a sense, this story marks a turning point in the Ramona stories—a turn to increasing sophistication of theme and the foreshadowing of Cleary's increasing preoccupation with the writing of stories that reflect her own conflicted attitude about the world: "Funny and sad, or even funny and tragic, describes my view of life."[9] Or, as she put it in her Newbery speech: "I find life humorous, sorrowful and filled with problems that have no solutions. . . ."[10]

While *Ramona the Pest* marks a tentative turning point in Cleary's writing career, it is, nevertheless, filled with the same kinds of humor that brightened *Beezus and Ramona*.

For example, the child's misunderstanding of words: Taught the words of the National Anthem, Ramona is (understandably) puzzled by the phrase "the dawnzer lee light," deciding, finally, that "a dawnzer was another word for a lamp." (It will be Ramona's turn to be embarrassed when Beezus taunts her about her misunderstanding.) A more dramatic example occurs when the teacher tells her to "sit here for the present" and Ramona refuses to budge until she gets her promised gift. When the mistake is explained to her, Ramona muses, "Words are so puzzling. *Present* should mean a present just as *attack* should mean to stick tacks in people" (p. 27).

Repetition is, again, a reliable source of humor: Every time Ramona sees her new classmate Susan, a girl with curls "like springs," she thinks "Boing." And, inevitably, she will simply *have* to pull on one of the curls and *say* "boing"—not once (once is never enough for Ramona) but twice. When other kids follow her example, Susan—being *that* kind of girl—runs to the teacher: "Miss Binney! Miss Binney! They're teasing me! They're pulling my hair and boinging me!" (p. 141).

There is also much humor to be found in Ramona's continuing demonstration that she may be the only little girl in literature who genuinely deserves the description "larger than life." When she's bad, she's very, very bad, and when she's good, she overdoes it: Determined to be "the best rester in the class" at nap time, "she gave one little snore, not a loud snore but a delicate snore, to prove what a good rester she was." Of course, everyone is soon snoring "except the few who did not know how to snore. They were giggling" (pp. 35–36).

As this suggests, situation is also a reliable source of humor, especially when it arises from character: Chapter 5, "Ramona's Engagement Ring," begins with Ramona's strident declaration "No! . . . I don't want to be sensible. . . . I hate being sensible!" (p. 102).

Being sensible, in this case, would mean wearing her friend Howie's hand-me-down boots to school. Ramona, as any child would understand, is determined *not* to do this. How she gets new boots, "beautiful red boots, *girl's* boots" (p. 111), and how they—and Ramona—wind up stuck in the mud, forcing a so-embarrassed-he-could-die Henry Huggins to go to her rescue, has not only a wonderfully funny air of humorous inevitability about it but also demonstrates Cleary's skill at comic scene building.

The third title in the series, *Ramona the Brave* (1973), demonstrates another similarity between Jane Moffat and Ramona. When Jane Moffat and her best friend, Nancy, have a falling out (Jane has stuck up for another girl instead of defending Nancy, who was in the wrong), Jane contemplates finding a new best friend in a girl named Clara Pringle, but ultimately discards that idea "because Clara did not have the bravery Nancy had." Similarly, when Nancy and Jane are reunited, Jane says to Nancy, "I suppose I should have stuck up for you." Nancy replies, "No. You were right. You stuck up for Beatrice even though you're my best friend. *That's bravery*" (emphasis added, *Middle*, p. 256). Even before *Ramona the Brave*, Ramona has established that bravery is an important part of her character—even if it is more often a manifestation of stubbornness than strength of character: "Tears came into Ramona's eyes, but she would not cry. Nobody was going to call Ramona Quimby a crybaby. Never" (*Pest*, p. 33). On the other hand, Ramona is often frightened, and the title *Ramona the Brave* is at least partly ironic.

The term "bildungsroman" may seem too weighty a word to apply to the Ramona books (buildungsramona?), but it is appropriate in the sense that the entire series can be viewed as one long work in which we observe the education of Ramona by her exposure to life and the problems of the world, and watch her grow (she does age over the life of the series) and develop as a character and as a human being with whom we can empathize and identify.

Ramona's development is much more convincing than that of the Moffat children. Indeed, when—toward the end of *The Middle Moffat*—Jane finds herself wondering if she and her siblings aren't growing up, the ways in which this is manifested seem less organic than imposed by the author. Granted, Sylvie is now "sweet sixteen," gets love letters, and is about to graduate from high school; Joey and Rufus have become enamored of that new electronic marvel, the wireless. But these are simply trappings. The characters who are busy with these external phenomena have not changed internally in any *demonstrable* way.

Ramona, however, does change through the experiences she encounters.

The series will change, too, because of an experience that—at first—might suggest yet another commonality with the Moffat series: Mr. Quimby—in the next Ramona book, *Ramona and Her Father*—will lose his job, and forever after the Quimbys will be "a family who had to worry about money" (*Ramona Forever*, 1984, p. 4). This fact of life will become the cloud inside the silver lining, the persistent twilight gloom obscuring the humor that had been so radiant.

The Moffats greet their poverty with, as has been previously noted, unfailing good cheer. Perhaps this is because they know—in an almost Pirandello-like way—that their creator (Eleanor Estes, not God—though to a fictional character the author would be God) will never let anything too bad happen to them. Consider what is possibly the bleakest of the Moffat stories, "The Coal Barge" (*Moffats*), in which Joey loses the family's last five dollars. "Joe knew he had never felt as miserable as this before in his whole life. . . . The other Moffats, knowing how miserable he was feeling . . . felt scarcely less miserable" (p. 185).

How does Mama react? Does she scold? Does she chide? Does

she wring her hands? Hardly. "Mama finally said, 'Well, if it's gone, it's gone. We'll manage somehow.'"

If Ramona had lost the five dollars (make it twenty-five dollars to factor in inflation), her parents would have wailed, "Oh, Ramona. How could you?" Mrs. Quimby would then have looked tired and Mr. Quimby would have looked worried and Ramona would have gone into a passionate reverie about how unfair the world is.

As the Ramona books become darker and darker (a fact made manifest when the books are read consecutively over a short period of time), Ramona will increasingly rage over the unfairness of things. (The seed for this element of her character has actually been planted as early as *Ramona the Pest*: "'It's not fair,' Ramona thought" [p. 37].)

In *Ramona and Her Father*, Ramona thinks, "Nothing was ever fair for second graders" (p. 101). In *Ramona and Her Mother*: "Grown-ups could get away with anything. It wasn't fair" (p. 57).

By *Ramona Quimby, Age 8* (1981), Ramona is "overwhelmed by the unfairness of it all." And in the latest (and perhaps last) of the Ramona books, *Ramona Forever*, Ramona's "overwhelm" has turned to rage: "Ramona seethed, angry at the unfairness of all that had happened" (p. 20).

One begins to understand the real source of Ramona's rage (though she doesn't) on the next page, where Ramona muses, "It isn't fair . . . *even though grown-ups were always telling her life was not fair*" (emphasis added). No wonder that, on the next page immediately following *that*, we find the phrase "In spite of her bitterness . . ."

In a sense, Ramona has become the victim of her parents' ever-diminishing expectations. It is almost pathetic that, as early as *Ramona and Her Father*, we find her crossing off all the presents she has written down on her Christmas list and printing, in their place, the one thing she now really wants: "One happy family."

As, in subsequent books, Mr. Quimby goes from failure to failure, becoming ever more discouraged and frustrated, Mrs. Quimby is depicted as becoming tireder and tireder, often disappearing to the privacy of her bedroom, retiring early or lying in bed reading. And when Ramona tries to cheer her family up by repeating something that used to make them laugh (calling tomatoes "tommy-toes"), Mr. Quimby reacts angrily: "Ramona, my grandmother used to have a saying. 'First time is funny, second time is silly, third time is a spanking'" (*Father*, p. 65).

So much, it would seem, for repetition as a humorous device.

Over the course of the series, then, Ramona goes from worry to defeat, from resentment to rage, and finally gives in to bitterness.

This does not pretend to be a psychoanalytic study (far from it), but it is surely significant to note that Cleary's own father lost his job when she was a girl, and thereafter her mother (like Mrs. Quimby) "sometimes worked outside the home. Her life was not easy and neither was mine, for I sometimes felt that *in her hurry and fatigue* [emphasis added] she did not have time left over for love."[11]

On another occasion, referring to her young self, Cleary has written, "I do not write solely for that child . . . I am also writing for my adult self . . . The feeling of being two ages at one time is delightful. . . ."[12]

It is not so delightful for the reader, however, when that adult point of view overpowers Ramona's own, a phenomenon that will occur increasingly as the tone of the series darkens.

At first this conflicted point of view comes across as self-pitying: In *Ramona the Pest*, Ramona thinks, of herself, "Poor little Ramona, all alone except for Ribsy behind the trash cans. Miss Binney would be sorry if she knew what she had made Ramona do" (p. 92).

Later it will manifest itself more didactically, as an adult "lesson" is layered onto a child's point of view: "[Ramona] thought about Susan who always acted big. In kindergarten there was no worse crime than acting big" (p. 164). Or: "People who called her a pest did not understand that a littler person sometimes had to be a little bit noisier and a little bit more stubborn in order to be noticed at all" (p. 162). Or this, from *Ramona and Her Father*: "Didn't grown-ups think children worried about anything but jack-o'-lanterns? Didn't they know children worried about grown-ups?" (p. 85). Or from *Ramona Quimby, Age 8*: "Grown-ups often forgot that no child likes to be ordered to be nice to another child" (p. 37).

This magisterial observation, like the ones preceding it, is presented as Ramona's but is all too obviously Cleary's own.

Finally, consider this (also from *Ramona Quimby, Age 8*): "The Quimbys' house seemed to have grown smaller during the day until it was no longer big enough to hold [Ramona's] family *and all its problems*" (emphasis added, p. 173).

So it is ultimately problems, not humor, that will prevail in the Ramona books (and in the Quimby household). If there were any lingering doubts about this, consider page 110 of *Ramona Forever*: Mr. Quimby, having finally finished college, discovers that he cannot find work as a teacher and, so, announces that he has accepted a job managing a supermarket. Beezus protests, "But you don't like working in the market."

To which her father bravely replies, "We can't always do

what we want in life, so we do the best we can."

"That's right," said Mrs. Quimby. "We do the best we can."

A bitter lesson for children to hear but not an unrealistic one. The sentence that follows, however, is almost unbearably sad: "Mr. Quimby's smile could not hide the discouraged look in his eyes."

One cannot help but wonder, in this context, about the last line of this last Ramona book: "[Ramona] was winning at growing up" (p. 182).

"Winning?" But, the reader may ask, hasn't Cleary just demonstrated that growing up is not about winning but, rather, about losing? Or, to put the best face on it, about settling? About compromising? About finding defeat in victory? All in all it is an oddly dispiriting and downbeat ending to what had started out as such a very high-spirited series!

The reader will have no such doubts, however, about the protagonists of another family series: Betsy Byars's indomitable Blossom kids—Junior, Vern, and Maggie—will clearly win at growing up despite having to overcome enough adversity and heartbreak and crisis to justify one reviewer's description of the first book about them as being "tragicomedy."[13]

Implicitly acknowledging this mixture of the muses in her work, Byars has said, "I am drawn to humor but I am not a humorist. My own books are serious with comic episodes. . . .The humor in my books serves a dual purpose. It balances out the serious things . . . It also humanizes things that are so dreadful they are in danger of dehumanizing us—wife abuse and child neglect, for example. The ability to laugh is the ability to put a distance between us, to give us the feeling we're still in control."[14]

The later Ramona books seem to lack that necessary distance, which is such a staple of the five Blossom books. The reason for this may lie in the different attitudes that Cleary and Byars bring to their respective material and the relative weight they assign to tragedy and comedy in their view of the world. For Cleary, tragedy (well, problems and misfortune, anyway) is heavier than comedy and ultimately outweighs the humorous. The attitude that prevails, thus, is serious—even, at times, oppressive.

For Byars it is just the opposite. Humor prevails. The tone is light. The reader's spirits are released from care and sent soaring like Junior Blossom's "Green Phantom." But wait, we're getting ahead of ourselves here.

The Blossoms first appeared in *The Not-Just-Anybody Family* (1986). They made their second appearance in *The Blossoms Meet the Vulture Lady* the same year (the first time in her long career Byars had written a sequel). The next two Blossom books—*The Blossoms and the Green Phantom* and *A Blossom Promise*—appeared in 1987.

Byars had promised that the fourth Blossom book would be the last, but four years later she broke that promise—to the delight of Blossom family fans—with the publication of a fifth title, *Wanted . . . Mud Blossom* (1991).

The Blossoms, like the Peppers and the Moffats, are a single-parent family. In their case, however, this is not a function of prevailing socioeconomics but of Byars's habit of cheerfully "getting rid of parents" as quickly as possible in her books, since she believes that how children on their own deal with problems is inherently more interesting than their dealings would be with the intervention of a supportive parent.[15]

In this case the father, Cotton, has been killed in a rodeo accident and the mother, Vicki, is a trick rider who is often absent, touring on the rodeo circuit. The resident adult, by default, is the children's grandfather, Pap, who is as prone to crisis as the kids are.

The family lives on a farm somewhere in the rural South, although they seem not to work the land they live on. Instead, Pap earns a living of sorts by driving around the countryside in his pickup truck collecting cans, usually in the company of his dog, Mud. The reader may infer that money is not a prominent fixture in the Blossoms' lives, but that fact is almost never mentioned, except when their mother worries about having enough money for new clothes to impress her latest boyfriend.

The adult reader's first reaction to the Blossoms is that they are refugees from a touring company of *Tobacco Road* (Pap even has a still in the basement). But Byars's skill at creating memorable (and, as importantly, *likable*) characters soon disabuses us of that notion.

From our first glimpse of Junior standing on top of the family barn wearing wings of "his own design," we realize that an important part of the series's unfailing humor will be these quirky characters themselves. What Byars says of Thorne Smith's character Cosmo Topper could be equally applied to the Blossoms: "the more familiar you become with him, the funnier he is, which may be the measurement of a truly humorous character."[16]

She goes on to define what she means by "humorous character": "I mean the individual in whom some particular quality is developed beyond those of his fellow man. . . . The true humorous character does not clash with reality. There has to be the element of plausibility or the result is a comic character, which is different."[17]

She cites as an example Mad Mary (the eponymous "vulture lady" of *The Blossoms Meet the Vulture Lady*), whom we will discuss in a moment.

But most readers will think Ralphie is the better example. Not a member of the Blossom family but a friend of theirs, Ralphie is one of the most gifted liars in children's literature. We first encounter him when Junior falls off that barn roof where we first encounter *him* and winds up sharing a hospital room with Ralphie.

At first Junior doesn't know why Ralphie is there. Ralphie chooses to enlighten him: "Here is what's really and truly wrong with me. I swallowed watermelon seeds and now watermelons are growing inside me, and when they get big, I'm going to bust open. . . . After I bust open, they're going to put a zipper in my stomach so I can zip myself open and shut" (p. 39).

"No" is all Junior can gasp in reply.

Although Ralphie mellows a bit after he meets Maggie Blossom and falls in love with her, it is still a laugh-out-loud funny moment when (in *The Blossoms and the Green Phantom*) we read, "Ralphie would do something so unusual, so refreshing his mother would be stunned. Ralphie would tell the truth" (p. 61).

In fact, Ralphie as a character reminds one of the gifted liars of the nineteenth-century frontier. Byars reinforces this point in *Wanted . . . Mud Blossom*, where we read what Ralphie has written about himself: "I am the fastest man on earth. I drive my bike up mountains without slowing down. I have been known to run to New York City and back during recess. I hold the world record for the Indy 500. To let off steam one Saturday afternoon, I dug a hole to China, had tea, and filled the hole back up in time for the family barbecue. When I am bored, I race eighteen-wheelers on the freeway" (p. 130).

Eat your hearts out, Davy Crockett and Mike Fink!

Ralphie's brag is, of course, intrinsically funny in its inspired hyperbole, but it is also touching when the reader remembers that, because of a mowing accident, Ralphie has an artificial leg (the real reason he was in the hospital was that he was being fitted with a new limb). Byars does not sentimentalize this fact; it is presented, simply, as a reality of Ralphie's life. It doesn't get in his way and it doesn't get in the reader's, either.

The Blossoms, themselves, of course, are not without their own . . . idiosyncracies. In *Wanted . . . Mud Blossom*, Maggie, explaining to Ralphie that Vicki's new boyfriend is coming for a visit, fumes, "We are to pretend we are a normal, everyday family, which we aren't! Maybe we can pretend to be normal for an hour or two, but not for a whole weekend. We Blossoms have never been just anybody" (p. 11).

One way Byars demonstrates this is by selectivity of the detail she chooses to share with the reader. We learn, for example, that Vern blew off half of a finger playing with dynamite when he was six. Later we learn that, while Junior dreams of becoming a stuntman, and Maggie a trick rider, Vern's most secret desire is to work in an office! "His happiest moments in school came when the teacher asked them to fill out forms!" (*Not-Just-Anybody*, p. 69).

As for Junior: "he loved for people to follow him, even to spy on him. It was flattering. . . . He loved to have to tell people again and again to leave him alone. His saddest moments were when they did" (*Vulture Lady*, p. 17). Indeed, his largest moments of frustration come when he tries every sort of elaborate device he can conjure up to keep his work-in-progress (i.e., another new invention) secret from prying eyes only to discover that no one is curious enough to even bother to pry.

We are also told that Junior loves to share (unlike most kids: "'I'm tired of sharing,' said Howie. 'Share, share, share. That's all grown-ups ever talk about. . . .' Ramona . . . understood exactly what he meant" [*Ramona the Pest*, p. 57]).

What Junior *really* wants to share, of course, is information about his inventions, in hope, the reader infers, that others will share something with him: their attention and their approbation.

Maggie, experiencing the unaccustomed pleasure of having a "comforting wad of money in her pocket" and being herself complimented by a stranger, feels "rich and special. She decided it was a great combination" (*Not-Just-Anybody*, p. 91). Maggie's domestic circumstances are sufficiently modest that, for her, getting to watch a man (on the hospital TV) dressed like a hot dog win a refrigerator can reasonably be described as "This was living" (!) (p. 105).

On a deeper level, of course, all these humorous details "balance out the serious things" (see above, p. 175). After all, doesn't Vern's secret desire suggest his longing for a more normal, ordered life? And doesn't Junior's suggest a longing for the kind of attention that is not forthcoming from his absent parents? And doesn't Maggie betray a reaction to a life of privation and, like Junior, a lack of adult approbation?

As for Mad Mary—Mary is a bag woman who lives, by choice, in a cave in the woods and dines on road kill du jour. "Mad Mary liked to get meat that hadn't been run over five or six times. It was juicier" (*Vulture Lady*, p. 8). This is funny, but it's not so funny when, in a subsequent book, Mary winds up in the hospital suffering from worms and malnutrition. And, though Byars has said she considers Mary a humorous character, she is anything but when we first meet her: "Mad Mary had not smiled in ten years. She hadn't seen anything to smile at. The big difference between animals and people, she had once read, is that people can laugh. Well, then, that meant she was more like an animal. It wasn't likely she would ever smile again, much less laugh" (p. 32).

Mary is one of what Byars calls her "vulnerable" characters. The others are Pap, Junior, Ralphie, and the dog, Mud. Things (which Byars calls "confusions" in her Sutherland Lecture) seem to happen to them. "Although confusion is a part of all the Blossoms' daily existence, it's somehow most humorous when it happens to these five."

This observation is offered in the context of what Byars calls "the humor of situation," which "arises out of confusion, mix-ups, blunders and misadventures."[18] How the characters deal with these "confusions" is more important than the action itself, according to Byars.

The introduction of such crises, the disintegration of order into disorder, is, of course, a classic recipe for humor. When it is coupled with character, the result is a higher humor called "comedy."

"Confusions" are necessary, of course, to drive the plots of what are the first real novels to be discussed in this chapter (the Moffat and Ramona books, although typically united by a tenuous theme, are too episodic to be considered true novels).

The structure of the Blossom novels involves the establishment of a main plot—usually revolving about one of Junior's ill-starred "inventions"—and at least two subplots, which may involve Pap's misadventures or those of Ralphie or Mary or even Mud: One of the drolleries of the Blossom books is that Mud's point of view is represented (nonanthropomorphically) along with that of the other Blossoms—no surprise to learn that Byars calls Mud "one of my favorite characters" and recalls that she has owned, at one time or another, more than twenty-eight different dogs.[19]

Byars then intercuts cinematically among these various plots, changing scenes at dramatic moments to build suspense and momentum and to draw the reader into the story. As might be imagined, repetition of incident enhances the humor (Junior is stuck on a barn roof at a moment of crisis in the first Blossom book, and again in the third book). Byars is well aware of the importance of this technique: "I use mostly repetition of event," she has observed. "In *The Blossoms Meet the Vulture Lady*, it's funny when Junior is trapped in the coyote cage. It's funnier when Mud is trapped in the same coyote cage. If I could have trapped two or three more Blossoms in the coyote cage, I would have, and it would have been funnier each time."[20] (This cage traps more than Junior and Mud, by the way: It also traps Byars into too baldly stating the theme of this book. Mary says to Junior, "I was about in a cage myself, and getting you out of yours was the start of getting me out of mine" [p. 128].)

Cages, literal or symbolic, provide a recurring theme of the Blossom books: Pap goes to jail in the first one and is trapped in a Dumpster in the third one; Ralphie gets trapped in dissembling; Mary is trapped in the hospital; Junior is trapped on a barn roof, etc. Liberation is the denouement of many of the books and may symbolically reinforce the free-spirited nature of the Blossoms and the liberating nature of the humor in the books about them.

Much of that humor is found in the jokes and one-liners, in the dialogue and the pithy observations that enrich and enliven all the books—the first books in this chapter to routinely employ such devices. Here are some examples:

Ralphie says to Junior, "You were probably lucky just to break two legs." "That's all I've got" is Junior's sorrowful (and literal-minded) reply (*The Not-Just-Anybody Family*, p. 28).

Later, Ralphie says, "Reporters try to take unflattering pictures. That's part of their training. They throw the good pictures in the trash can" (p. 102).

Ralphie's mother owns a balloon shop and is being undercut by a rival balloon business that delivers—in costume: "Every time [Ralphie's] mom saw a gorilla driving through town with a backseat filled with balloons, it drove everything else out of her mind" (*Green Phantom*, p. 59).

Ralphie threatens his younger brother: "You will end up splattered all over Mom's car, and you know how particular she is about the Blazer" (p. 60).

Ralphie's mom promises, "Ralphie, if your brothers are in that box, your life as a happy person is over!" (*Wanted*, p. 66).

Ralphie calls his mother "The Ogress." When he inadvertently tells Maggie that she reminds him of his mother, she charges, "You think I'm an ogress?" He, thinking fast, replies, "No, you're more like an—oh, I don't know—an ogrette. . . . That's a small ogress," he adds helpfully, "like a dinette or kitchenette" (*Wanted*, p. 22).

The best one-liner, however, because it so perfectly captures the spirit of the series, is this: "The emergency numbers are on the first page [of the telephone book]," Junior comments. Pap's reply: "Seems like that's the only numbers we ever need around here" (*Wanted*, p. 49).

Writers are seldom the best judges of their strengths and weaknesses, but Betsy Byars is an exception. Consider what she identified as "the two talents" she started with as a beginning writer:

"1. An ease with words (which came from a lifelong habit of reading) and

"2. An ease with dialogue (which came from being born into a family of talkers)."[21]

As the Blossom books demonstrate, Byars does have an easy facility for creating readable prose. Her style never gets between her and the reader—which is not to say her prose is styleless, only that it never self-consciously calls attention to itself. An important element of this style is, as she suggests, her use of dialogue. How her characters say a thing is sometimes as important as what they say. And certainly, as the above examples evidence, dialogue is a very important part of the humor of the five Blossom books. An equally important part, however, is what might be called monologue. Byars's writing voice—her tone—is very similar to her own speaking voice: natural, unaffected, and humorous. Anyone who has heard her speak would not doubt for a second the truth of her claim that she was born into a family of talkers. For a writer, this is a wonderful gift and one that seems to have been given to many Southern writers: It is why we think of them as natural storytellers. Since Byars employs the omniscient point of view in writing (or "telling") the Blossom stories, her tone when the omniscient narrator is speaking is an important consideration, since it is a reflection of her own worldview, which is, as was discussed earlier, intrinsically humorous.

Byars is being a bit disingenuous when she says she is "not a humorist." The overriding attitude that informs almost all of her books—not just the Blossom series—*is* humorous. One understands why she claims that her books are "serious with comic episodes," for every humorous writer wants to be taken seriously, as we have discussed elsewhere in this book. But nowhere is it clearer than in the Blossom books that it is Betsy Byars's great gift to write humorous books . . . with serious episodes!

Another writer who has a great talent for mixing serious and comic elements in her work is Lois Lowry, who most clearly demonstrates this talent in the Anastasia Krupnik books.

Of the first title in this splendid series, *Anastasia Krupnik* (1979), the critic Zena Sutherland writes, "The writing is lively, funny, and above all, intelligent"[22]—an appraisal that can be applied, without reservation, to the other volumes: *Anastasia Again!*, 1981; *Anastasia at Your Service*, 1982; *Anastasia, Ask*

Your Analyst, 1984; *Anastasia on Her Own*, 1985; *Anastasia Has the Answers*, 1986; *Anastasia's Chosen Career*, 1987; and *Anastasia at This Address*, 1991. There are also two books about Anastasia's little brother, Sam: *All About Sam*, 1988, and *Attaboy, Sam!*, 1992.

Unlike the Blossoms, the Krupniks are an urban family, living near Boston (the Quimbys are also urbanites, living in Portland, Oregon, but their milieu seems much more that of small-town America). Myron Krupnik is a professor at Harvard University and a National Book Award–winning poet. Katherine Krupnik is a children's book illustrator, and their house is filled with books and music (ranging from Mozart to Billie Holiday). They are loving, supportive parents who actually enjoy talking with their children (and with each other), and, *mirabile dictu*, they are perhaps the only fictional adults in this chapter who have a sense of humor!

What Jean Fritz has written about Betsy Byars can, I think, be equally applied to Lois Lowry: "Whenever I finish a book by Betsy Byars, I have an overwhelming urge to put a star beside the title along with the code letters P.I.—Parents Invited."[23]

This thought occurs to me because Lowry brings to the Anastasia series a worldview that, like Byars's, is essentially humorous and that manifests itself in ways that are amusing to both children and adults.

The Krupniks' lives are hardly devoid of the world's larger dilemmas—if death, divorce, senility and other problems of aging, physical disfigurement, skull fractures, and other such tribulations can be called dilemmas—but the point is made, again and again, though *never* didactically, that humor is the grace that, in their wake, saves us from despair.

Professor of education and storyteller Eric Kimmel has

observed that "No writer in the field of children's literature wears both tragic and comic masks as well as Lois Lowry."[24] This inevitable interconnectedness of the tragic and comic is probably most vividly demonstrated in the two strongest of the Anastasia books: the first, *Anastasia Krupnik*, and the sixth, *Anastasia Has the Answers*, both of which, in different ways, deal with death.

In the former, Anastasia, then ten, must come to grips with her grandmother's advancing senility and ultimate death. In the latter—Anastasia is now thirteen—it is her aunt who has died (not an inevitable death from old age but an unexpected death from food poisoning at a cruelly young age).

Though handled very differently, the two deaths are exercises in self-discovery and important benchmarks in Anastasia's emotional growth and emerging maturity.

At first, for example, Anastasia thinks she hates her grandmother, who is ninety-two and lives in a nursing home: "Nobody else's grandmother was ninety-two. Robert Giannini's grandmother was fifty; she played the Hammond Organ in a bar and lounge" (p. 58). (Note the added humor in the superfluous detail of its being a Hammond Organ.)

Anastasia's conflicted emotions about her grandmother color her feelings about the elderly in general and are the reason, she decides, that she dislikes her teacher, Mrs. Westvessel: "'I think Mrs. Westvessel is probably over one hundred years old,' Anastasia told her parents at dinner" (p. 5). Since everyone else in the class likes the teacher, however, Anastasia sadly decides that the real reason she doesn't is that she is dumb, "because sometimes—too many times—I don't feel the same way about things that everybody else feels" (p. 7).

Gradually, however, Anastasia discovers that her feelings about her grandmother are more complex than she had realized—

"It was a feeling of being scared and sad at the same time" (p. 55).

Having discovered this, Anastasia then has a moment of emotional epiphany when her grandmother arrives for a Thanksgiving visit: "'I don't hate Grandmother,' she said in a voice that had to find its way out lopsided, around the tears. 'I hate it that she's so old. It makes my heart hurt'" (p. 62).

What she means, and what the reader understands, of course, since it has been carefully dramatized by Lowry, is that it's not her grandmother's age that Anastasia hates but what aging has done to her grandmother. To leave it at that might make the grandmother seem pathetic or victimized, however, and so Anastasia will find another revelation about her grandmother, this time, gratifyingly, in a work of literature: Anastasia visits one of her father's poetry classes at Harvard. In a wonderfully satirical scene— although satirizing college students is like shooting fish in a barrel—Anastasia discovers, through her father's explication of the Wordsworth poem "I Wandered Lonely as a Cloud," that her grandmother has "the inward eye, the bliss of solitude" in her happy memories. Accordingly, when her grandmother dies soon thereafter, Anastasia's *own* memories are both sad and happy. And there is both art and wisdom in Lowry's treatment of these sensitive issues.

There is, of course, a sad inevitability about the death of someone who is ninety-two years old. There is not inevitability but shock about the sudden, unexpected death from food poisoning of Anastasia's fifty-five-year-old aunt Rose in *Anastasia Has the Answers*. Shock . . . and fear. After a good deal of dithering, Anastasia decides not to fly to California with her parents for the funeral. Later in the evening she explains why: "I was scared." Not of flying, she explains but of "—yuck, I even hate the word— *funerals*" (p. 5). When her mother reminds her that she hadn't been scared of her grandmother's funeral, Anastasia explains that this is different because of "The *age* thing, for one." And . . . "'The other thing.'"

"'Other thing?' her mother asked.

"Anastasia cringed. 'I don't quite know how to say it. Cause of Death.'"

"Salmonella?" Dr. Krupnik offers.

Anastasia's reaction this time is an even more resounding "YUCK!" She explains: "It sounds like someone's name. A mobster. A hit man. My Aunt Rose was killed by Sal Monella" (pp. 5–6).

This, of course, is irreverent—as both wordplay *and* attitude—but also funny. And healthy. We are as scared of death—especially when it sneaks up on us and surprises us—as Anastasia is. To laugh diminishes the fear by making it smaller, by putting distance between us and the fear of death.

Death gets laughed at a lot in this book. Not only in the personification of Sal Monella but in three-year-old Sam's reaction. Anastasia discovers him, with a long line of his Matchbox cars, playing funeral. The scene (p. 37) is too long to quote, but it involves the parade of cars going to the sedentary ("Cemetery," Anastasia corrects) and a G.I. Joe filling in for Aunt Rose ("'And they bury her, like a tulip bulb. Goodbye, dead Aunt Rose,' Sam said.") (The point should probably be made, at least parenthetically, that the humor works here not only because of its irreverence but because of another kind of distance: the reader's from the character of Aunt Rose, whom we have never met and about whom we know almost nothing. Indeed, Anastasia and Sam are almost equally unfamiliar with their aunt, who lives a continent away).

The treatment of death aside, there is other, gentler irreverence in this book, too. Anastasia is musing about her favorite book, *Gone with the Wind*, and thinking that Ashley and Melanie are "kind of wimpy. . . . If they had lived in current times, Melanie probably would have worn lace-up shoes. Ashley would have gone to the symphony instead of rock concerts—just like Anastasia's father, who was occasionally pretty wimpy himself in a lovable sort of way" (p. 13). (In *All About Sam*, Dr. Krupnik self-deprecatingly calls himself "Mr. Flabbo." Sam says, "Good old Mr. Flabbo. I love you" [p. 121].)

Noticing that her "ancient, elderly" English teacher (he's "probably about sixty" [p. 34]) wears clear nail polish, Anastasia imagines him at home at night, grading papers and "polishing his nails at the same time, holding them up to see how they looked, blowing on them so they would dry. It seemed," she concludes, "very weird" (p. 34).

Such irreverence also helps Anastasia deal with her friend Daphne's problems. Another girl, Meredith, sighs, "Poor Daph. I wish her problems would go away." "Yeah, me too," Anastasia agrees. "But it would take a U-Haul van to haul them off, she has so many" (p. 14).

Daphne herself is irreverent. Finding Anastasia in the garage practicing rope climbing (there *is* a compelling plot purpose for this), Daphne says, "Honestly, Anastasia, if my mother was in the garage with a rope around the rafters, you *know* she wouldn't be practicing rope climbing" (p. 28). In context the reader understands that Daphne is talking, in an irreverent way, about suicide. All of this is funny. But some of it is only a chuckle away from tragedy. That we can view it as humor is, in part, due to the distancing effect of our irreverent laughter, but also to our not dwelling too—well—*seriously* on the reality of the situations that engage our emotions and imaginations.

Anastasia herself understands this, as is demonstrated in a later Anastasia book, *Anastasia at This Address*, in which Anastasia muses about a TV news report she has seen of a collision between a mail truck and a truckload of chickens. "Peter Jennings made it sound like a funny event. . . . But I didn't find it at all amusing. For one thing the chickens looked very scared, and the people chasing them didn't look too thrilled either."

In a sense empathy is one of humor's worst enemies.

So is sentimentality, and Lowry's view of the world is refreshingly unsentimental. Anastasia agonizes over having a crush on her female gym teacher. Finally she goes to her mother in a typically adolescent way of asking for help: "I know this girl at school. . . . You don't know her. You never met her. You don't even know her name."

Mrs. Krupnik, of course, immediately understands that Anastasia is talking about herself but has the wisdom not to say so. Anastasia then unburdens herself. Mrs. Krupnik's response is to put her arms around her daughter and, carefully avoiding mawkishness, to tell Anastasia about her own teenage crush on her music teacher, Miss Hermione Fitzpatrick.

"*Hermione?*" Anastasia demands (and the reader chuckles).

"Sorry about the name," Mrs. K. replies, and goes on to reassure Anastasia that "this girl" is "not weird at all." Instead "she's very normal, very sensitive, very capable of loving" (p. 51–52).

Anastasia is reassured, and sentimentality—and adolescent angst—go down for the count.

A number of the other humorous devices that Lowry employs are similar to those that have been discussed above in the context of other authors' work. There is, for example, abundant wordplay (no surprise in books where the family works *New York Times* crossword puzzles), some of the funniest being double entendres: Anastasia wants to get her ears pierced and tells her father she's going to have a "lobotomy." Sam, overhearing his mother wishing he were "trained," thinks of the little engine that could.

Similarly, funny names and humor inspired by names are consistently reliable devices. In the very first book Anastasia's parents promise that she may name the new baby—an attempt at defusing the anger she feels over their "betrayal" of her by failing to consult her before deciding to have a second child ("the rats!" [p. 20]). Anastasia plots her revenge, writing in her notebook the most awful name she has ever heard. The reader does not, at first, know what this is, and so the suspense builds as the baby's arrival approaches. Then we find out the name: "One-ball Reilly" (which *may* be funnier to adults than to kids). Ultimately, artfully, Lowry arranges for the baby to be named Sam, in honor of his late grandfather. In the same book Anastasia grouses about her own name because it's too long to go on a T-shirt: "Into the *armpits*, right? The letters would go right into my armpits!" (p. 52). This sets her parents to fondly recalling people with names like "Weatherly Scarf" and "Felicity Brest" (an artist's model!).

The elderly lady next door is named Gertrude Stein, and Sam will routinely call her "Gertrustein." Anastasia is upset that her boyfriend Steve is calling her funny names: "Anapest," "Anastomosis." Sam says, "You could call *Steve* something bad." "Like what?" Anastasia demands. "Dog doo," he suggests (with, it might be added, perfect three-year-old logic and love for the humor of "forbidden" words [*Anastasia on Her Own*, p. 9].)

Superiority humor is another staple: Anastasia, trying to be sophisticated, politely asks an adult dinner companion who has declined a glass of wine, "Is that because you're a recovering alcoholic?" (*Anastasia at This Address*, p. 101). More often the superiority is of the self–put-down variety: Anastasia, striving for the fashionable "layered" look, decides she looks like a bag lady or a sausage instead.

There is even occasional sarcasm: Anastasia tells her father that because a number of foreign educators will be visiting her school, all the students are supposed to be "real patriotic and happy and enthusiastic and uplifting." His reply: "Like Nazi Youth?" (*Anastasia Has the Answers*, p. 85).

If humor is truth, Lois Lowry is one of the greatest truth tellers in children's literature. Truth and humor have in common their spontaneity; their candor, their freedom from cant and artifice. They are found in an author's attitude toward her or his material and characters. They are expressed in the tone of a work and captured in its spirit. For me the spirit of the Anastasia series is perfectly captured in another of Anastasia's observations. Her uncle George has just said, of Daphne, "she has the most beautiful hair. It reminds me of Shirley Temple."

"Oh, gross," Anastasia thinks. "Elderly people like Uncle George [he's in his late fifties]—and even Anastasia's parents—all liked those old Shirley Temple movies, where she danced around, smiling, showing her dimples—and sometimes her underpants, talk about *gross*—with her curls bouncing" (*Anastasia Has the Answers*, p. 72).

She then recalls that Daphne has once done a Shirley Temple impersonation for a school talent assembly but while wearing a black-lace garter belt and with one of her front teeth blacked out.

"The entire junior high had thought it was hysterical. . . . But everybody over the age of thirty-five . . . thought it was sacrilegious or something . . ." (p. 72).

Shirley Temple fans may think Daphne's send-up is sacrilegious (and I can't even imagine what Rufus M. or Eleanor E.

would think), but contemporary kids may recognize that it dramatizes how popular enthusiasms change over time. And it may even cause them to wonder how children of a future generation will view *their* enthusiastic embrace of the likes of a Macauley Culkin.

On another occasion Dr. Krupnik comforts Anastasia, who has gotten an F on a poem she has written, by explaining that some people "just haven't been educated to understand poetry" (*Anastasia Krupnick*, p. 17).

With wonderful wit, emotional honesty, and humor's saving grace, the Anastasia books artfully offer an education in understanding the world.

Humor in the American family story has obviously come a very long way since the days of *Little Women*. The Anastasia books are a wonderfully secure home in which to leave it.

Notes

[1] Crouch, Marcus, *The Nesbit Tradition*. London: Ernest Benn Limited, 1972, p. 179.

[2] Faragher, John Mack, *Daniel Boone*. New York: Henry Holt and Company, 1992, pp. 49–50.

[3] Griswold, Jerry, *Audacious Kids*. New York: Oxford University Press, 1992, pp. 157, 165.

[4] Meigs, Cornelia, et al., *A Critical History of Children's Literature*. New York: The Macmillan Co., 1953, p. 540.

[5] Hiss, Tony, "Really Rosie," *The New Yorker*, LXVIII:70 (January 18, 1993).

[6] Landsberg, Michele, *Reading for the Fun of It*. New York: Prentice Hall Press, 1987, p. 61.

[7] Cleary, Beverly, "The Laughter of Children," *The Horn Book*, LVIII: 560–61 (October 1982).

[8] Cleary, Beverly, "Newbery Medal Acceptance," in *Newbery and Caldecott Medal Books 1976–1985*, edited by Lee Kingman. Boston: The Horn Book, Inc., 1986, p. 126.

[9] Cleary, "Laughter," p. 558.

[10] Cleary, "Newbery," p. 130.

[11] Cleary, Beverly, "Regina Medal Acceptance," in *Children's Literature Review*, vol. 8, edited by Gerard J. Senick. Detroit: Gale Research Company, 1985, p. 36.

[12] Cleary, "Laughter," p. 558.

[13] Kenney, Susan, review of *The Not-Just-Anybody Family*, *The New York Times Book Review*, June 15, 1986, p. 38.

[14] Byars, Betsy, "Taking Humor Seriously," in *The Zena Sutherland Lectures: 1983–1992*, edited by Betsy Hearne. New York: Clarion Books, 1993, pp. 213–14.

[15] Personal interview with the author, February 1986.

[16]Byars, "Taking Humor Seriously, " p. 212.

[17]Byars, "Taking Humor Seriously, " p. 223.

[18]Byars, "Taking Humor Seriously, " p. 223.

[19]Personal interview.

[20]Byars, "Taking Humor Seriously, " p. 219.

[21]Byars, Betsy, *The Moon and I*. Englewood Cliffs, N.J.: Julian Messner, 1991, p. 32.

[22]Sutherland, Zena, review of *Anastasia Krupnik*, *Bulletin of the Center for Children's Books*, 33:99 (January 1980).

[23]Fritz, Jean, review of *The Night Swimmers*, *The New York Times Book Review*, May 4, 1980, p. 26.

[24]Kimmel, Eric A., "Anastasia Agonistes," *The Horn Book*, LXIII:182 (March/April 1987).

Afterword

CONFABULATION AND CLOSURE

I knew several essential things about humor when I started writing this book; others I learned in the process. One thing I knew at the outset was that life is not easy for kids. The world is as often too much with them as it is with us adults. And so laughter, as a means of at least temporarily escaping from the oppressions of the world, is as essential for them as it is for grown-ups. It releases their tensions, too, and helps calm their fears. It even heals their emotional wounds.

Kids may not consciously understand that, but they intuitively look for books that will make them laugh. I loved the Freddy the Pig books when I was a kid because *they* made me laugh. As an adult, I can look back from the distance of middle age and realize that the Freddy books may even have saved my life. Norman Cousins is not the only one to have found laughter a life-or-death proposition.

Because humor is such a powerful agent for redemption, it needs to be taken *very* seriously. And that is its fundamental irony.

I wish humorous books were taken more seriously by critics and presenters of glittering prizes, if it is true that one of the functions of criticism and award giving is to encourage the publication of good books, for we need more good humorous books for children. After all, there are still lives to be saved, but unfortunately the light-spirited in literature continues to be treated as if it were lightweight! It's wryly amusing to consider that the Newbery Medals won by Betsy Byars, Beverly Cleary, and Lois Lowry recognized their "serious" work and not the kinds of humorous works that have made them so enormously popular and that continue to command the love of their readers.

I think "love" is a good word to use here. It certainly helps explain why so many adult readers take the favorite humorous books of their childhoods so seriously, uncritically treasuring the books that lightened the burden of their own childhoods, that ensured at least a small place for play in the serious and dangerous day-to-day of growing up.

And speaking of play: Here's something I learned in writing this book. It had never occurred to me until I read Max Eastman that to enjoy the humor of a story one must approach it in a state of mind that he called "in fun"; that is, the kind of mind-set children experience when at play. This leads me to the thought that laughter is like a piano: It needs to be practiced. Both the ivories and the sense of humor need to be tickled. The more they are, the easier it will be for an adult to recapture that spirit of fun, to lighten up!

Happily the varieties of humorous experience are numerous, ranging from surprise to tickles, from jokes to school-yard chants, from funny names to forbidden words. But the most genial of these experiences, I believe, is the reading of a genuinely humorous book. The late Alvin Schwartz put it better than I ever could: "There are times when we laugh out of the sheer pleasure of encountering the work of a humorously creative mind, whether words or illustration are involved . . . what is critical is whether you are in a playful mood . . . a playful response evokes laughter. . . ."[1]

Ah, laughter! If the sublime has a sound, it is that of laughter. I am as sure of that as I am sure that heaven is the experience of being surrounded by enough humorous books so that you can, as Josh Billings put it, "laugh until your soul is thoroughly rested."[2]

What a good thought with which to end a book about humor.

Notes

[1] Schwartz, Alvin, "Children, Humor and Folklore, Part I," *The Horn Book*, LIII:282 (June 1977).

[2] Quoted in Schwartz, Alvin, "Children, Humor, and Folklore, Part II," *The Horn Book*, LIII:476 (August 1977).

Selected Bibliography

PRIMARY SOURCES

Alcott, Louisa May. *Little Women*. Boston: Roberts Brothers, 1868–69.

Atwater, Richard and Florence. *Mr. Popper's Penguins*. Boston: Little, Brown, 1938.

Bennett, John. *The Pigtail of Ah Lee Ben Loo*. New York: Longmans, Green, 1928.

Bowman, James Cloyd. *Pecos Bill*. Chicago: Albert Whitman & Company, 1937.

Brooks, Walter R. *The Clockwork Twin*. New York: Knopf, 1937.

———. *Freddy and Mr. Camphor*. New York: Knopf, 1944.

———. *Freddy and Simon the Dictator*. New York: Knopf, 1956.

———. *Freddy and the Baseball Team from Mars*. New York: Knopf, 1955.

———. *Freddy and the Bean Home News*. New York: Knopf, 1943.

———. *Freddy and the Dragon*. New York: Knopf, 1958.

———. *Freddy and the Flying Saucer Plans*. New York: Knopf, 1957.

———. *Freddy and the Ignormus*. New York: Knopf, 1941.

———. *Freddy and the Men from Mars*. New York: Knopf, 1954.

———. *Freddy and the Perilous Adventure*. New York: Knopf, 1942.

———. *Freddy and the Popinjay*. New York: Knopf, 1945.

———. *Freddy and the Space Ship*. New York: Knopf, 1953.

————. *Freddy Goes Camping.* New York: Knopf, 1948.

————. *Freddy Plays Football.* New York: Knopf, 1949.

————. *Freddy Rides Again.* New York: Knopf, 1951.

————. *Freddy's Cousin Weedly.* New York: Knopf, 1940.

————. *Freddy the Cowboy.* New York: Knopf, 1950.

————. *Freddy the Detective.* New York: Knopf, 1932.

————. *Freddy the Magician.* New York: Knopf, 1947.

————. *Freddy the Pied Piper.* New York: Knopf, 1946.

————. *Freddy the Pilot.* New York: Knopf, 1952.

————. *More To and Again.* New York: Knopf, 1930. Reissued as *Freddy Goes to the North Pole*, 1949.

————. *The Story of Freginald.* New York: Knopf, 1936.

————. *To and Again.* New York: Knopf, 1927. Reissued as *Freddy Goes to Florida*, 1949.

————. *Wiggins for President.* New York: Knopf, 1939. Reissued as *Freddy the Politician*, 1948.

Byars, Betsy. *A Blossom Promise.* New York: Delacorte Press, 1987.

————. *The Blossoms and the Green Phantom.* New York: Delacorte Press, 1987.

————. *The Blossoms Meet the Vulture Lady.* New York: Delacorte Press, 1986.

————. *The Not-Just-Anybody Family.* New York: Delacorte Press, 1986.

————. *Wanted . . . Mud Blossom.* New York: Delacorte Press, 1991.

Cleary, Beverly. *Beezus and Ramona.* New York: Morrow, 1955.

————. *Ramona and Her Father.* New York: Morrow, 1977.

————. *Ramona and Her Mother.* New York: Morrow, 1979.

————. *Ramona Forever.* New York: Morrow, 1984.

————. *Ramona Quimby, Age 8.* New York: Morrow, 1981.

————. *Ramona the Brave.* New York: Morrow, 1973.

————. *Ramona the Pest.* New York: Morrow, 1968

Estes, Eleanor. *The Middle Moffat.* New York: Harcourt, Brace, 1942.

———. *The Moffat Museum*. New York: Harcourt, Brace, 1983.

———. *The Moffats*. New York: Harcourt, Brace, 1941.

———. *Rufus M.* New York: Harcourt, Brace, 1943.

Fleischman, Sid. *By the Great Horn Spoon!* Boston: Little, Brown, 1963.

———. *Chancy and the Grand Rascal*. Boston: Little, Brown, 1966.

———. *Humbug Mountain*. Boston: Little, Brown, 1978.

———. *Jingo Django*. Boston: Little, Brown, 1971.

———. *McBroom Tells the Truth*. New York: Norton, 1966.

———. *Mr. Mysterious and Company*. Boston: Little, Brown, 1962.

———. *The Whipping Boy*. New York: Greenwillow Books, 1986.

Gág, Wanda. *Millions of Cats*. New York: Coward, McCann, 1928.

Grahame, Kenneth. *The Wind in the Willows*. London: Methuen & Co., 1908.

Kellogg, Steven. *Johnny Appleseed*. New York: Morrow, 1988.

———. *Mike Fink*. New York: Morrow, 1992.

———. *Paul Bunyan*. New York: Morrow, 1984.

———. *Pecos Bill*. New York: Morrow, 1986.

Lawson, Robert. *Ben and Me*. Boston: Little, Brown, 1939.

———. *Captain Kidd's Cat*. Boston: Little, Brown, 1956.

———. *I Discover Columbus*. Boston: Little, Brown, 1941.

———. *Mr. Revere and I*. Boston: Little, Brown, 1953.

———. *They Were Strong and Good*. New York: Viking Press, 1940.

Leaf, Munro, *The Story of Ferdinand,* New York: Viking, 1936.

Lobel, Arnold. *Days with Frog and Toad*. New York:, Harper & Row, 1979.

———. *Frog and Toad All Year*. New York: Harper & Row, 1976.

———. *Frog and Toad Are Friends*. New York: Harper & Row, 1970.

———. *Frog and Toad Together*. New York: Harper & Row, 1972.

Lofting, Hugh. *Doctor Dolittle and the Green Canary*. Philadelphia: Lippincott, 1950.

————. *Doctor Dolittle and the Secret Lake*. Philadelphia: Lippincott, 1948.

————. *Doctor Dolittle in the Moon*. New York: Stokes, 1928.

————. *Doctor Dolittle's Caravan*. New York: Stokes, 1926.

————. *Doctor Dolittle's Circus*. New York: Stokes, 1924.

————. *Doctor Dolittle's Post Office*. New York: Stokes, 1923.

————. *Doctor Dolittle's Garden*. New York: Stokes, 1927.

————. *Doctor Dolittle's Puddleby Adventures*. Philadelphia: Lippincott, 1952.

————. *Doctor Dolittle's Return*. New York: Stokes, 1933.

————. *Doctor Dolittle's Zoo*. New York: Stokes, 1925.

————. *Gub Gub's Book*. New York: Stokes, 1932.

————. *The Story of Doctor Dolittle*. New York: Stokes, 1927.

————. *The Voyages of Doctor Dolittle*. New York: Stokes, 1922.

Lowry, Lois. *All About Sam*. Boston: Houghton Mifflin, 1988.

————. *Anastasia Again!* Boston: Houghton Mifflin, 1981.

————. *Anastasia, Ask Your Analyst*. Boston: Houghton Mifflin, 1984.

————. *Anastasia at This Address*. Boston: Houghton Mifflin, 1991.

————. *Anastasia at Your Service*. Boston: Houghton Mifflin, 1982.

————. *Anastasia Has the Answers*. Boston: Houghton Mifflin, 1986.

————. *Anastasia Krupnik*. Boston: Houghton Mifflin, 1979.

————. *Anastasia on Her Own*. Boston: Houghton Mifflin, 1985.

————. *Anastasia's Chosen Career*. Boston: Houghton Mifflin, 1987.

————. *Attaboy, Sam!* Boston: Houghton Mifflin, 1992.

Malcolmson, Anne. *Yankee Doodle's Cousins*. Boston: Houghton Mifflin, 1941.

McCloskey, Robert. *Centerburg Tales*. New York: Viking Press, 1951.

————. *Homer Price*. New York: Viking Press, 1943.

————. *Lentil*. New York: Viking Press, 1940.

————. *Make Way for Ducklings*. New York: Viking Press, 1941.

Rounds, Glen. *Ol' Paul, The Mighty Logger.* New York:Holiday House, 1936.

Shephard, Esther. *Paul Bunyan.* New York: Harcourt, Brace, 1924.

Sidney, Margaret (Harriet M. Lothrop). *Five Little Peppers and How They Grew.* Boston: Lothrop, 1881.

Sketches and Eccentricities of Colonel David Crockett of West Tennessee. New York: J. & J. Harper, 1833.

Twain, Mark. *Adventures of Huckleberry Finn.* New York: Charles L. Webster, 1885.

——. *The Adventures of Tom Sawyer.* Hartford, Conn.: The American Publishing Company, 1876.

SECONDARY SOURCES

Alexander, Lloyd. "No Laughter in Heaven." *The Horn Book,* XLVI:11–19 (February 1970).

Apte, Mahadev L. *Humor and Laughter.* Ithaca, N.Y.: Cornell University Press, 1985.

Arbuthnot, May Hill. *Children and Books.* Chicago: Scott, Foresman and Co., 1947.

Bader, Barbara. *American Picturebooks from Noah's Ark to The Beast Within.* New York: Macmillan, 1976.

Beckson, Karl, and Arthur Ganz. *Literary Terms: A Dictionary.* New York: The Noonday Press, 1989.

Blair, Walter. *Native American Humor (1800–1900).* New York: American Book Company, 1937.

——. *Tall Tale America.* Chicago: The University of Chicago Press, 1987.

Blishen, Edward. *Hugh Lofting (Three Bodley Head Monographs).* London: The Bodley Head, 1968.

"Bothering to Look: A Conversation Between Robert McCloskey and Ethel Heins." In *Innocence and Experience*, edited by Barbara Harrison and Gregory Maguire. New York: Lothrop, Lee & Shepard, 1987.

Botkin, B. A. *A Treasury of American Folklore*. New York: Crown, 1944.

Byars, Betsy. *The Moon and I*. Englewood Cliffs, N.J.: Julian Messner, 1991.

———. "Taking Humor Seriously." In *The Zena Sutherland Lectures: 1983–1992*, edited by Betsy Hearne. New York: Clarion, 1993.

Cart, Michael. Interview with Betsy Byars, March 10, 1987.

Cart, Michael. Interview with Sid Fleischman, February 9, 1987.

Cleary, Beverly. "The Laughter of Children." *The Horn Book,* LVIII:555–64 (October 1982).

———. "Newbery Medal Acceptance." In *Newbery and Caldecott Medal Books 1976–1985*, edited by Lee Kingman. Boston: The Horn Book, 1986.

———. "Regina Medal Acceptance." In *Children's Literature Review,* vol. 8, edited by Gerard J. Senick. Detroit: Gale Research, 1985.

Crouch, Marcus. *The Nesbit Tradition*. London: Ernest Benn, 1972.

Daugherty, James. "Homer Price: Comment by Eric Gugler and James Daugherty," *The Horn Book*, XIX:424–26 (November 1943).

Dorson, Richard M. *America in Legend*. New York: Pantheon, 1973.

Eastman, Max. *Enjoyment of Laughter*. New York: Simon & Schuster, 1936.

Egoff, Sheila A. *Worlds Within*. Chicago: American Library Association, 1988.

Erdoes, Richard. *Tales from the American Frontier*. New York: Pantheon, 1991.

Eyre, Frank. *British Children's Books in the Twentieth Century*. New York: Dutton, 1971.

Faragher, John Mack. *Daniel Boone*. New York: Henry Holt, 1992.

Fenner, Phyllis. *The Proof of the Pudding.* New York: The John Day Company, 1957.

Fish, Helen Dean. "Robert Lawson—Illustrator in the Great Tradition." In *Caldecott Medal Books: 1938–1957*, edited by Bertha Mahony Miller and Elinor Whitney Field. Boston: The Horn Book, 1957.

Fisher, Margery. *Who's Who in Children's Books.* New York: Holt, Rinehart and Winston, 1975.

Fleischman, Sid. "Laughter and Children's Literature," *The Horn Book,* LII:465–70 (October 1976).

Fritz, Jean. Review of *The Night Swimmers. The New York Times Book Review*, May 4, 1980, p. 26.

Griswold, Jerry. *Audacious Kids.* New York: Oxford University Press, 1992.

Grotjahn, Martin. *Beyond Laughter.* New York: McGraw-Hill, 1957.

Gutwirth, Marcel. *Laughing Matter.* Ithaca, N.Y.: Cornell University Press, 1993.

Heins, Ethel. "A Cry for Laughter," *The Horn Book,* LV:631 (December 1979).

Hiss, Tony. "Really Rosie," *The New Yorker,* LXVIII:70–71 (January 18, 1993).

Hobbes, Thomas. *Leviathan.* Edited by Michael Oakeshott. Oxford: Basil Blackwell, 1960.

Inge, M. Thomas. *The Frontier Humorists.* Hamden, Conn.: Archon Books, 1975.

Inman, Sue Lile. "Robert Lawson." In *Dictionary of Literary Biography,* vol. 22, edited by John Cech. Detroit: Gale Research, 1983.

Jones, Helen L. *Robert Lawson, Illustrator.* Boston: Little, Brown, 1972.

Kappas, Katherine H. "A Developmental Analysis of Children's Responses to Humor," *The Library Quarterly,* 37:67–77 (January 1967).

Kenny, Susan. Review of *The Not-Just-Anybody Family. The New York Times Book Review*, June 15, 1986, p. 38.

Kesterson, David B. "West." In *American Humor: A Historical Survey*

(*Dictionary of Literary Biography*, vol. 11, part 2), edited by Stanley Trachtenberg. Detroit: Gale Research, 1982.

Kimmel, Eric A. "Anastasia Agonistes." *The Horn Book*, LXIII:181–87 (March/April 1987).

King, Jessica. "Freddy the Detective" (Review). *Library Journal*, 57:865 (October 15, 1932).

Landsberg, Michele. *Reading for the Fun of It*. New York: Prentice Hall, 1987.

Lauber, John. *The Making of Mark Twain*. New York: American Heritage, 1985.

Lawson, Marie A. "Master of Rabbit Hill—Robert Lawson." In *Newbery Medal Books: 1922–1955*, edited by Bertha Mahony Miller and Elinor Whitney Field. Boston: The Horn Book, 1955.

Lawson, Robert. "Acceptance Paper." In *Caldecott Medal Books: 1938–1957*, edited by Bertha Mahony Miller and Elinor Whitney Field. Boston: The Horn Book, 1957.

———. "Acceptance Paper." In *Newbery Medal Books: 1922–1955*, edited by Bertha Mahony Miller and Elinor Whitney Field. Boston: The Horn Book, 1955.

———. *At That Time*. New York: Viking Press, 1947.

———. "Make Me a Child Again." In *Something Shared: Children and Books*, edited by Phyllis Fenner. New York: The John Day Company, 1959.

Lewis, C. S. *The Four Loves*. New York: Harcourt, Brace, 1960.

Lobel, Arnold. "A Good Picture Book Should . . . " In *Celebrating Children's Books*, edited by Betsy Hearne and Marilyn Kaye. New York: Lothrop, Lee & Shepard, 1981.

Lofting, Christopher. "Afterword." In *The Voyages of Doctor Dolittle* by Hugh Lofting (The Centenary Edition). New York: Delacorte Press, 1988.

McCloskey, Robert. "Caldecott Medal Acceptance." In *Newbery and*

Caldecott Medal Books: 1956–1965, edited by Lee Kingman. Boston: The Horn Book, 1965.

———. "Ducklings at Home and Abroad." In *Caldecott Medal Books: 1938–1957*, edited by Bertha Mahony Miller and Elinor Whitney Field. Boston: The Horn Book, 1957.

Meigs, Cornelia, et al. A *Critical History of Children's Literature*. New York: Macmillan, 1953.

Moore, Anne Carroll. *My Roads to Childhood*. New York: Doubleday, Doran, 1939.

———. "The Three Owls' Notebook." *The Horn Book,* XXV:116 (March/April 1949).

Natov, Roni, and Geraldine DeLuca. "An Interview with Arnold Lobel." *The Lion and the Unicorn,* 1:72–96 (1977).

"On an Author." (Walter R. Brooks) *New York Herald Tribune Book Review,* November 15, 1953, p. 2.

Opie, Iona and Peter, eds. *I Saw Esau*. Cambridge, Mass.: Candlewick Press, 1992.

O'Reilly, Edward J. "The Saga of Pecos Bill." *The Century* LXXXIV:827–33 (October 1923).

Painter, Helen W. "Robert McCloskey: Master of Humorous Realism." In *Authors and Illustrators of Children's Books*, edited by Miriam Hoffman and Eva Samuels. New York: Bowker, 1972.

Rourke, Constance. *American Humor: A Study of the National Character*. New York: Harcourt, Brace, 1931.

Schmidt, Gary D. *Robert McCloskey*. Boston: Twayne, 1990.

Schwartz, Alvin. "Children, Humor, and Folklore, Part I." *The Horn Book,* LIII:281–87 (June 1977).

———. "Children, Humor, and Folklore, Part II." *The Horn Book,* LIII:471–76 (August 1977).

Shannon, George. *Arnold Lobel*. Boston: Twayne, 1989.

Simont, Marc. "Bob McCloskey, Inventor." In *Newbery and Caldecott*

Medal Books: 1956–65, edited by Lee Kingman. Boston: The Horn Book, 1965.

Smith, Dora V. *Fifty Years of Children's Books*. Champaign, Ill.: National Council of Teachers of English, 1963.

Suhl, Isabelle. "The 'Real' Doctor Dolittle." In *The Black American in Books for Children: Readings in Racism* (2nd ed.). Metuchen, N.J.: The Scarecrow Press, Inc., 1985.

Sutherland, Zena. Review of *Anastasia Krupnik*. *Bulletin of the Center for Children's Books*, 33:99 (January 1980).

Tave, Stuart Malcolm. "Humour." In *Encyclopedia Britannica*, vol. 11. Chicago: Encyclopedia Britannica, 1972.

Townsend, John Rowe. *Written for Children* (3rd rev. ed.). New York: J. B. Lippincott, 1987.

"Two Authors." *Utica Observer Dispatch*, February 1, 1938, p. 12.

"Walter R. Brooks." Knopf promotional brochure, n.d. (ca. 1945).

Watson, Ernest W. *Forty Illustrators*. Freeport, N.Y.: Books for Libraries Press, 1970.

White, E. B., and Katharine S. White, eds. *A Subtreasury of American Humor*. New York: The Modern Library, 1941.

Wolfenstein, Martha S. *Children's Humor: A Psychological Analysis*. Bloomington: Indiana University Press, 1978.

Yolen, Jane. "Fleischman, (Albert) Sid(ney)." In *Twentieth-Century Children's Writers* (3rd ed.), edited by Tracy Chevalier. Chicago: St. James Press, 1989.

Index